IDEOLOGY

Influences and Trend of the Naga Political Movement

IDEOLOGY

Influences and Trend of the Naga Political Movement

Dr. Ringkahao Horam

Sunmarg Publishers & Distributors
H.No. 36, Maidan Garhi, New Basti,
Post IGNOU, New Delhi-110068

Published by:
Sunmarg Publishers & Distributors
H.No. 36, Maidan Garhi, New Basti,
Post IGNOU, New Delhi-110068
Mob: +91-9717502501
Email: sunmargpublishers@gmail.com

First Edition : 2016

IDEOLOGY: Influences and Trend of the Naga Political Movement

ISBN 978-93-82606-41-3

Typesetting by :
J.K. Graphics (India)
Shahdara, Delhi

PRINTED IN INDIA

Digital Printing by RK Offset Process, Naveen Shahdara, Delhi-110032
Mob: 9810080542

Preface

The world is in a constant flux, nothing is static. In this dynamic world, everything revolves along with time and circumstances marching forward and thinking of better future. However sometimes someone, somewhere, something goes wrong and affects the system, which compels to regenerate and redress again. The Naga Political movement is one of them.

Honestly admitting the limitation of my knowledge, with courage I have taken decision to write something on the Naga political Movements which was a burning issue since my childhood days.

In the teaching profession for more than 25 years, I had the opportunity to interact with many students in different categories. It is very interesting to see the youngsters, trying their best to learn and cope up the latest of everything that encounters them. However, it is so discouraging to find many youngsters not knowing even the basic knowledge about our heritage; like history, culture, political movements, etc. This motivated me to write on such topics. Here I have tried my best to be lucid in writing so that even the least educated persons and students or those who are new to the Nagas' political problem may be able to understand without much difficulty.

Secondly, most of the Naga Political movement's important documents are not available. Here, I try my best to enclose as many as possible for others to have access through this publication.

This book may not be written in scientific and scholarly approach, for which, it may need lots of modifications, however, with the above stated reason I venture to publish it, believing the system that "all great things begin from small one".

I do not claim my work as the most genuine and authentic one. However I simply and honestly present the facts without any prejudice.

In Part 1of this book I have written about the Ideology : influence and trend of the Naga political movement

In Part II Chapter I, I have given the historical backgrounds of the Nagas, like origin and migration waves of the Nagas, and the Nagas relations with Ahoms and the British.

In Chapter II, I have written mainly about the factors responsible for the Naga political movements such as Nationalism, Fear psychosis, social economic set up, exploitation, religious impact and Political consciousness, etc.

In Chapter III, I have discussed about the Naga Political history since the formation of the Naga Club in 1918. I have also briefly discussed the Simon Commission and also given the Crux of the Naga political problem. This is followed by the formation of the NNC and the movements under the leadership of Phizo.

Chapter IV is about the different Agreements and Accords reached between the two parties and their impacts.

In Chapter V, I have written about the present trends and the formation of the NSCN and its aims and objectives.

Lastly, I have discussed the overall assessment of the Movements and their impacts.

Dr. Ringkahao Horam

Introduction

In a country with an enormous size like India where there are diversities of people following different social, cultural and religious beliefs, it is difficult for the people to know each other. Today, through science and technology, communication has improved to a great extent. This seems to bring the world and the people nearer to one another. Yet, within the same country we are not aware of things that are happening around us.

Some years back, when we said 'Naga', denoting the name of a tribe, very few people knew it. But today, all of us, especially in North-east India know the Nagas. Yet many people are not aware of the social and the political history of the Nagas and their problems. The political movement of the Nagas is one of the oldest political movements in India. However, this political movement of the Nagas is deliberately, coined as underground, hostile, extremist, terrorist or outlawed activities, etc. without actually knowing the real nature of the movement.

It is true that before the coming of the British, the Nagas were not united as one. However there was a sense of oneness among the Naga community. They lived in the state of nature, the knowledge of state or Nationality was not known to them. Every village was more or less independent like that of the Greek-city state. Therefore, the Nagas or their land did not belong to any bigger country.

Thus, historically, the Nagas argued that they were not a part of India.

The British had classified the land inhabited by the Nagas as "excluded area ". This was because the British thought that the Nagas were quite different from the rest of the Indians. Thus, the British kept the Nagas under a separate category. The British policy towards the Nagas in the later part was reformation and uplift mend rather than destruction, or exploitation. In fact, the British did not rule the Nagas. They rather took care of them.

Then the question arises as to how the land inhabited by the Nagas was integrated as a part of India. There are arguments for and against the process of integration into the Indian Union. This is the main theme that I would like to deal in this book.

To the Nagas, the early period was a stage of Golden period. Then the British period was a period of progress and peaceful transformation from tradition to modernization. The third period began after India's Independence. The period is marked by confusion, trouble and unrest. In fact the seeds of nationalism were already sown in the minds of the Nagas during the British rule. The impact of Christianity and modern education strengthened the spirit of nationalism among the Nagas.

Today, even after more than 50 years of the political struggle, the Naga problems are yet to be solved. The Naga problem is gaining its momentum day by day. Therefore, this should not be treated merely as law and order problem.

To understand the Naga political issue, we must understand the historical facts. History involves not only the mere record of facts, but it needs an interpretation of facts. We cannot twist the exact history. But we can certainly unearth the buried facts of the past. History is a continuous process from generation to generation, drifting along with our free mental rational flow. So, in order to understand a complicated issue like Nagas political movement, one should know the roots of the Naga political movement.

My presentation in this book will be more of analytical than descriptive as many documents are available on this topic. Lastly, the Naga political problem is quite sensitive and touchy. Moreover, it is quite complicated issue, but let the historical fact remain unchanged and let it speak out boldly and honestly.

Contents

PART–I

Ideology: Influences and Trend of The Naga Political Movement

1
Ideology: Influences and Trend

1.1. IDEOLOGY

Ideology is a system of political, legal ethical aesthetical, religious and philosophical views and ideas.

It is loosely defined as "belief system". The political ideology is a set of political beliefs that characterize any group, individual, government or the entire nation.

A political ideology is "a programmatic and rhetorical application of some grandiose philosophical system, which arouses men to political action and may provide strategic guidance for that action"[1]

(a) Its linkage with a grand philosophical system

(b) Its program contents derived from its philosophy

(c) Its strategy of achieving the programmatic goal and

(d) The coverage of its following (what groups or how much of the population subscribes to it)[2]

Fundamentally ideologies are programs for action and instruments of evaluation. There are mainly four important functions of ideologies[3], they are:

1. To evaluate distribution and exercise of political power and the working of political institutions.
2. To rouse people to action and to mobilize political movements.
3. To Provide a distinctive language or vocabulary to facilitate the process of examination of political regime and
4. To "provide some mental organization for the frequent confusion of political life.

The 17th and 18th Century of industrial revolution leads to famous French Revolution in 1789. It is true that most of today's ideologies are mainly consequences and reactions of this great revolution. Ideology is dynamic and is never static. It moves along with the social, economic and political situation, belief and faith of that people, when societies are in crisis, socially, economically or politically looking for better future. Ideology is assumed as savior, as a guiding force to deliver from the crisis. Usually the new political realities have to be accommodated with the passage of time.

Liberalism is considered as the philosophy of the bourgeois class, *Marxism* as the philosophy of the working class, *evolutionary socialism* as the philosophy of social democrats and *Fascism* as the philosophy of reactionaries, which try to save the crisis created by capitalist system. In this process, man is the main actor, and centre in which all the socio-economic and political system revolve around it and the ideology provide an explanation of human nature.

According to Lewis S. Fever, there are three ingredients in ideology "the first, an invariant myth, the second, a compound of philosophical doctrine which alternate cyclically in the history of ideology, the third, and a historically determined decision as to a chosen class of the time. These three ingredients, as invariant mythological structure, an alternating set of philosophical tenants, and a historically determined chosen group are inherent in every ideology."[4]

Lewis further gives two important mythological ingredient of ideology. He said that, the mythological ingredient is essential to ideologies; without it their historical use and attractive power cannot be understood. The two mythological theories are:

1.1 (a) The Mosaic Revolution Myth

This myth is taken from Holy Bible in the book of Exodus. It is about the story of Moses who struggle to liberate Hebrew Tribes. It is said that the Mosaic myth is invariant through all ideological transformation.

"The Mosaic myth can be stated in its most elemental form as a series of situation and incidents:

1. A people is oppressed;
2. A Youngman not himself of the oppressed people;
3. Moved by sympathy, he intervenes, and strikes down an oppressor's henchman;
4. He flees, or goes into exile;
5. He experiences the call to redeem oppressed people;
6. He returns to demand freedom for the oppressed;
7. He is spurned by the tyrannical ruler;
8. He leads the actions which after initial defeats overwhelm the oppressor;
9. He liberates the oppressed people;
10. He imparts a new sacred doctrine, a new law of life, to his people;
11. The newly liberated people relapse from loyalty to their historic mission;

12. Almost disillusioned, their leader to re-educate them morally for their new life;
13. A false prophet arises who rebels against the leader's authoritarian rule, but he is destroyed;
14. The leader, now he revered law giver, dies as he glimpses from afar the new existence.[5]

The Mosaic myth is about the Youngman intellectual revolution who has been witnessing the hardship of his people who are socially, economically and politically suppressed and exploited. He was clear of his ideology and with selfless and dedication he moves forward for the cause of the exploited. He suffers exile and imprisonment; but he leads his people to historic victory. But his people are still slavish in their psychology, and incapable of realizing the new society. So he has to still lead his people from front upholding his ideology; he deal with factional elements; he dies, with the sight of the new Promised Land; his people lived remembering his deed. Thus, the Mosaic myth shows the mythological ingredient is essential to ideologies.

Karl Marx wrote that "The present generation is like the Jews, whom Moses led through the wilderness. It has not only a new world to conquer it must go under, in order to make room for the men who are fit for a new world".[6]

This Mosaic myth not only gives revolutionary spirit but also give moral strength to the struggle. This mythological ingredient is essential to ideologies.

1.1 (b) The Jacobic Myth of the Elect

The second type of myth which is taken from the Holy Bible of the Old Testament which we might call it as "The Jacobic Myth, it is taken from the Book of Genesis Chapter 27. This Biblical myth revolve around the theme: Who will inherit the birthright? Who will have the father's blessing? In this story Jacob conspires with the help of his mother to deprive his brother Esau of the birthright, for it will decide who will be chosen among the peoples. "The Jacobic myth narrates simply:

1. There was a father with several sons;
2. The sons contended for the father's blessing, which would determine their place in the world's hierarchy in future time;
3. The intellectual son, the younger, is forced by his brothers to undergo ordeals;
4. The intellectual, younger son secures the historic birthright.

Whereas the Mosaic myth is one of revolt against the Pharaoh the established order, the Jocobic myth clarifies the nature of the historic mission; the intellectual favored son is fulfilling the mandate of a higher established order. The revolutionary son is exculpated, for he is indeed the most conservative, the most obedient to the primal mandate. The primary content of the Mosaic myth is revolt against injustice; that of the Jocobic myth is the emergence of a new elite or new class, in the political cosmos".[7]

When we closely examine this two Biblical mythological ingredient, and correlate with the different ideologies and revolution, it is one way or the other closely associated. The main source and foundation of Naga political movement and its ideology are based in Biblical mythology particularly based in Mosaic myth and revolution. They have political, spiritual and ideological inspiration from the story of Israel people. Where they are subjected to enslavement, socially discriminated, economically exploited and politically suppressed. But under the leadership of Moses he once again rises up and liberates his people from the oppressed.

Naga political ideology are so much deeply rooted in the Spiritual Biblical Myth that in 1960s onward it give its slogan "Nagaland for Christ" and make it the core objective of its movement.

1.1 (c) End of Ideology: Utopia or Reality

Origin of the Theory

In Italy at Milan in September 1955, there was a conference of "Western intellectual"–The congress for cultural freedom in which more than 150 intellectual, mostly thinkers, politicians and journalists participated. The main issue that they discussed in this congress was "how to secure future freedom in western societies" and what should be the methods adopted so that they maintain free and open society. Most of the participants give opinion that there should not be any ideological conflicts in the free society. Therefore "End of Ideology" is required for free and opens society. So they enclosed the concept of "End of Ideology". This was follow by many other sociological and economic concepts emerged, such as "Single Industrial Society" "Stages of economic Growth" "Convergence Theory" "Post Capitalist Society" and Value-Free Social Science"[8]

All this concepts are associated with the theory of "End of Ideology".

Just after the Second World War there emerged many newly independent countries, in Asia, in Africa, and in Latin America etc. These newly formed countries could be one of the alliances of the two super powers either communist bloc lead by USSR or Democratic block lead by USA. This ideological rivalry and conflict leads to dividing the world into two power block which result into emergence of new "War" known as "Cold War". It is not a physical war but an

"Ideological War", which actively show up from 1945-1955. This was the period where some of the western intellectual contemplating to have "End of Ideology" because the world cannot allow to have another war because they have had bitter experience in the past two destructive world war. Secondly some of this theorist believed that the western societies are "Post-Capitalist Societies", here it argue that the working class has socio-economic and political rights and there is no exploitation of the working class in this societies. It further said that the class conflict is these societies are over and social class harmony is established. Therefore the role of ideology is limited and diminishing hence they propagate the "End of Ideology".

In America during the regime of Kissinger while formulating US foreign policy he try to propagate "End of Ideology" and attempted to strengthen relation with USSR and China which were considered as rival Ideological bloc. This end of ideology is attempted so as to have "Peaceful Co-existence" and mutual tolerance to liberalism and Marxism. It also argued that in course of time, liberalism and Marxism have changed-Liberalism in the radical direction and Marxism in the bureaucratic direction, and because of this change, both the ideologies have lost their original positions, hence fading the significance of ideology.

But the "End of Ideology" cannot be a reality, because without ideology, all social and political activities remain purposeless, and ideology itself is meaningless if it cannot act as a guide to the social activities of men. Some of the industrialized and developed countries advocate "End of Ideology" but almost all the underdeveloped or third world countries do not accept this theory. Thus for working class end of ideology means end of revolution, which means end of way to "Liberalism". End of ideology is mainly advocated by USA and UK but here in these two countries they have bi-party system which does not have ideological conflict. Because of this, ideology becomes less significant for them.

It will be wrong to assume and generalized their perception. Today the roles of ideology become more and more significant and more so for the third world countries. It is a guiding force and root of human political being.

The role of ideology in the Naga political movement since their inception has deeply rooted. But it is true that they do not have specific refine ideology, they are scatter mostly undefined, and no writer or scholar have so far written about it. But they are practice and vibrant, in their everyday life and their political movement. It lies in the form of customary law, culture and religion.

Secondly, the role of different ideologies in Naga political movement seems to swing from one to another according to time and circumstances.

Thirdly traditional way of life particularly customary law and culture are backbone of its ideology which stands firmly from the beginning till now.

Fourthly, religious ingredient and its spirit linger throughout their movement and their aspiration.

Fifthly, the Naga political movement has an ideology of "Christology" where Jesus Christ is the symbol of justice, love, peace and liberty. Therefore it has a slogan and objective of "Nagaland for Christ".

Sixthly, Mosaic myth of revolution and ideology is made the foundation and basis of the Nagas movement. They personify Nagas as Israel, the chosen people of God, who were delivered from the oppressor, with the help of God.

Considering the above points, let us discuss some of the ideology: influences and trend of Naga political movement.

1.2 (a) Gandhism and the Nagas

Mahatma Gandhi who was a saint like political leader of India, who was given a title "Father of the Nation", came in to the political scene when India needed him most. Gandhi era (1918-1947) was one of the most crucial periods in the political movement of India.

It was a period where no political leader could bring unity of the masses, where British have sown the seed of animosity and follow the principle of divide and rule policy.

Apart from his political ideology some of the main contributions of Gandhi are:

1. Hindu Muslim Unity,
2. Removal of untouchability,
3. Raising the social status of women in India.

Gandhi do not want to call his ideology as Gandhism, had he been alive now he would never allow people to address him as "Mahatma" because he is such a humble man, who care for simple living, pious honest and holy life rather than making self exalted life. With such deep understanding meaning and purpose of life, he entered into the Indian political scene with non-violence as his main tools as an ideology. For him there is no politics without religion, therefore religion is part and parcel of all his ideology. Satyagraha or holding on to the truth is another ideology of Gandhi. He said when you follow non-violence and hold on to the truth you will have power of the soul. For him non-violence means not hurting 1) physically, 2) mentally, 3) spiritually.

For Gandhi religion is a way of life. His religion is not formal or customary in nature. He has varied practical approach to religion. His religion was pursuit of truth through love and service to individual. He also believes and advocates the system of decentralization, where maximum autonomy is to be given to the unit. Panchayati Raj or local self government which we have now is of his idea. The non-cooperation movement, civil disobedience movements are some of his tool for the political struggle.

Now the question often ask is how this head hunter the "Naga" who are branded as savage, barbarian by some writer was the admiral of the Gandhism. Seems to be strange but true "Nagas" are not barbarians, or savage, they have the most civilized sense of war. All their activities including war are governed by customary law no one dare to violate it because the consequences and the punishment is severe. Historically there is no record that Nagas are subjugated by war or forced. But there is history that Naga can be conquered by love and affection. Spreading of Christianity through love and affection was enough to conquered Nagas spiritual life within few year of time.

Gandhiji with his religious tone with the message of brotherhood, following non-violence and upholding the truth was enough to be attracted to his ideology. Naga has also seen how the mighty British bow down before Gandhi's simple ideology. He has proved the world that Gandhi's non-violence is mightier and more powerful than the British strongest weapon. Naga also have seen how Gandhi has brought the divided Indian masses into one irrespective of caste, class, creed, religion, or sex.

When Naga leader meet Gandhi in Delhi he assured them that the Naga has every right to decide of their future either to be part of India or Independent of their own. Such understanding and effectiveness of his ideology influence the Nagas. Therefore up to 1955 Nagas were following the ideological line of Gandhism. Even today Gandhi is one of the admired ideologue of the Nagas.

1.2 (b) Democracy

Democracy is a form of Government. Its concept and popularity is growing; therefore it became a key political ideal of the present century. Now it is not only form of government but a way of life. Though initially democracy was a political principle, now in the course of time it has been enlarged to include economic, social, and even ethical ideals.

Democracy was originated in Greece, this we can find in the writing of some of the great Greek philosophers. The name itself democracy is derived from the Greek word *demos* and *cratia*, meaning people and power. Thus literally democracy means the system of government in which the power rests with the people. But the concept and the practice of democracy in those days has been considerably changed. In those days democracy was only mean for the royal and ruling class, where the slave people were not allowed to exercise or involve in this governmental system. But the basic principles of the theory and its concrete shape are given by some of the western political thinkers in 17 century.

Mainly by Hobbes, Locke, Rousseau, Bentham, J. S. Mill etc. It was Hobbes who first wrote the democratic principles in his book call LEVIATHAN. Locke further elaborated the liberal theory of democracy and rule of law. Rousseau further contributed the principles of natural equality of men and right of the individual. Mill and Bentham also contributed to the theory of democracy by emphasizing the principles of adult franchise, representative, government, freedom of press, and election etc. Therefore the present form of democracy is a growth. Professor Seeley rightly describes democracy a "Government in which everyone has a share" But the most simple and popular definition is given by Abraham Lincoln which he describe democracy as "a government of the people, by the people and for the people". In spite of democracy the most popular form of government it is not free from criticism, it has many demerits too. But still it is consider as the best form of government.

Nagas were immensely influenced by western democracy. They were living a secluded life for thousands of years. They have their own world following their traditional culture and customary law. Their outside contacts were the advent of British and the Christian Missionaries in the late 19th Century and early part of the 20th Century. The seclusion and isolation from the outside world was over in the coming of the II World War. The Nagas through the II World War has opened their eyes and started seeing the outside world, their social and political life. They were impressed by the form of government that the British follow, particularly, the rule of law. Hence, Nagas are greatly influenced by the western democracy.

1.2 (c) Traditional Nagas National Democracy

The Nagas lived in villages; each village is like that of Greek city-state, 'a sovereign state'. Each Naga village was independent of other village. In those days, since their wants are limited, they managed whatever they have so they were self sufficient. J.P. Mill wrote thus, each village is independent unit in the tribes... in the days when villages were constantly at war each village was ruled by a chief assisted by an informal council of elders.[9]

The village chief is the head of the village. He usually performs two main functions: (a) as a religious head, (b) as a secular head, but there are some religions duties which are to be performed by the village priest. As a head of the administration his duty was to summon and preside over the meetings of the village councilors, who are usually represented from the various clans according to the custom.

The village administration is run well represented from each and every clan. While village chief is the head of the administration, democratic procedures were strictly maintained. Therefore, the king in no way can act as dictator, but his conduct and decision are to stick on the line of customary law and the wishes of the majority who are present in the meeting. The representative character of the council, the democratic procedures of administration and decision and the selection of the chief is a clear proof of democracy in Traditional Naga's Society. "Most Naga tribes are democratic in nature and govern themselves through a set of customary codes of conduct and laws, of ancient tradition. Though unwritten, these laws are well understood and per sued by the village and tribal councils. Among the Ao and Angami, these councils are formed by the village elders or chieftains and function as Justice Court against crime. The process of meeting out justice is supple, quick and based on the criminal sense to have erred", to sum up the administration of Naga society. Dr. V. Elvin has said that, "Naga society presents a varied pattern of near dictatorship and extreme democracy".[10] Therefore exactly modern form of democracy may not be there in Naga society, but the elements, ingredient procedures and spirit of democracy were there and practiced by the Nagas since time immemorial.

1.2 (d) Marxist Socialism

Karl Marx is known as the Father of Modern Socialism. He was critical of the Capitalist society which is based on exploitation, he wanted to create a society which is free from exploitation, a society in which everyone live in peace, harmony and have opportunity to develop self personality without any hindrance. Marx opined that socialism is also an ethical revolt against the terrible de-humanizing process involved in the institution of capitalism where it is based on competition in the market and survival of the fittest. Capitalism has reduced human being into a kind of commodity, which leads to self-alienation. The aim of socialism is therefore emancipation of human being, restoration of his self identity and creating a security based on equality. In short the characters of Marxian socialism are:

1. Marxian socialism opposed capitalism because it operates against the interest of the working class.
2. Marxian socialism gives more importance to the social good rather than the individual.
3. Marxian socialism opposed competition of production because it over produce and waste.
4. Marxian socialism opposed private property because it brings social class which is the root of social disharmony.
5. Marxian socialism believes in the principle of equality and positive freedom.

In the Communist manifesto, which he published in 1848 contains the basic main ideology of Karl Marx in which he not only show the emergence of social class and exploitation but also showed the way and means to overthrow the bourgeoisie class. With this small revolutionary tract, the world was shaken and new ideology, new concept based on social, economic and political were emerged.

Marxian socialism immensely influenced the Naga leader of the Naga political movement because it has shown some of the communist country developed drastically.

But at the same time some Nagas have apprehension because they think that the Marxist socialism may hinder their religious beliefs. But Marxism and Religion are two separate things which never mix because for Karl Marx, it is 'politics minus religion.' Throughout the ideology of Naga political movement, we can see some Marxian socialism lingering in one way or the other.

1.2 (e) Traditional Naga National Socialism

Socialism is political and economic theory advocating state or community ownership and control of means of production, distribution and exchange or social system based on equal sharing and on the principle of social, economic and political equality. If it is so, then the Naga traditional practice has all the elements of socialism.

Nagas are community-based social group. Each and every village is more or less independent. They lived their life in socialistic pattern of society. There is no social class and they do not differentiate between rich and poor. All citizens enjoyed equal rights, equal opportunities and they enjoyed freedom under village administrative system.

"The communist principle of economic equality was obtained in the Naga village-states. Whether it be construction of 'Fame-House' of stone dragging ceremony, the endeavors and gains were collective in nature. The rich freely shared their riches with the poor and the poor contributed freely their labors to the rich helping out each other whole-heartedly".[11]

The villager's activities are knitted as a whole whether religious life, social life, economic life or political life. In times of fishing, hunting and farming are mostly done in group or in community and whatever they got from hunting or fishing, they shared it equally. When they brought vegetables or any fruits from the farm or forest, the neighbors would have their share in it; when any person is fortunate to be rich, he will never become selfish but he automatically plan to throw party in form of 'feast of merit' where all the villagers will be fed for days with plenty of foods and drink served.

The Nagas not only have community-based social lifestyle and sharing of what they have, but they also have common holding of property like land. "In areas other than those where there was terraced and wet cultivation field, there was the system of owing the lands by the general public. The village council decides the particular areas where the Jhum cultivation could be done in a particular year. In Jhumming system, therefore, the entire land belonged to the people very much conforming to the principle of public ownership of land under the communist system. Individuals, however, could own small gardens and private woodlands for their own".[12]

To conclude, when we closely observe the Nagas traditional way of life and compare it with Marxian socialism, there are many similarities. In fact, Nagas traditional way of life is in socialistic pattern which has been practiced from time immemorial. Even today the Nagas are proud of their political heritage and practice them with beliefs that it is the best system for self and society for their growth and harmony.

1.2 (f) Christian Socialism

Christian socialism immerged in the first half of 19th Century which advocates class harmony. It believes that there is possibility of blending Christian ideas with Socialism. These Christian ideas are mostly taken from the Gospel book of Holy Bible. It aimed social reformation through moral perfection. These social doctrine are supported by many churches, thus they have formed Christian Trade Union and many other organizations. Christian socialism and Capitalism viewed socialism as realization of humanistic aspiration and they tried to adjust their religious belief to socialist ideal. Christian socialism also advocates social reformation through spiritual transformation.

The community life of the Christian also acts as a moralizing agent. The Naga Christian community life is based on Christian socialism. The community life was the index of their economic and social life. The spirit of oneness and corporate faith binds them together. Even today the Naga community life based in Christian socialism is the binding force and bed-rock foundation of social, economic and political movement of the Nagas.

1.3 NAGAISM

Nagaism may not be a distinctive or scientifically laid down doctrine like that of socialism, communism, Hinduism, Buddhism, etc. But it is a set of principles that has been voluntarily and automatically followed by the Nagas from the time immemorial. In other word it is "the way of life" of the traditional Nagas. For the Nagas, Nagaism is an article of faith which has been bestowed to them and follows from generation to generation. It is something like divine guiding force which makes a unique way of life.

In the Holy Bible, in the book of Genesis 1: 27, it said "God created man in his own image, in the image of God created him".[13] Therefore, according to Christian faith the natural man was a divine man. But because of the fall of Man (Adam and Eve fall into the temptation of Lucifer), Man become sinful. Hence the natural man who is sinless, blameless and divine being is lost. No human being is perfect and free from any sin.

Nagas are not exception to it but in spite of natural man who has lost his divine being, there seems to be natural man's elements which can be vividly seen in some of the tribe living isolated in the remote areas, where so call 'modern civilization' has not yet spoiled among them; the traditional Nagas is one of them. Therefore, they can be one of the fine specimens of humanity who may represent the "Natural Man".

"To the Nagas, man is by nature a corporate animal, always seeking the help of others. Every man is born for every other man and nobody is born for himself. Man is therefore, not only social by nature but also helpful to one another and help and cooperation are the absolute norm which makes their society harmonious. The social harmony and progress are expressed in the form of village-state.[14]

The Naga forefathers, when they came in the present abode were imbued by the divine spirit and they were determined to find future for themselves. Their activities and way of life were guided by the 10 basic virtues. The 10 virtues, the basic pillars of the Traditional Nagas are:[15]

1. Simplicity
2. Honesty and Truthfulness
3. Straight-forwardness
4. Generosity
5. Helpfulness
6. Regards for others
7. Religious
8. Fearlessness
9. Hard working
10. Rule of Law

1. Simplicity

The Nagas in the olden days were simple. Their needs were also limited. Injustice as such was not there. They have no other avenue to invest if they have any surplus also. They gather and store food grains for a year. They domesticated animals and if there is any surplus they share to the villagers in the form of 'Feast of Merit'. They were self-sufficient and they were contended with whatever they have. They were simple man, simple living and simple thinking. They do not worry for tomorrow. Whatever they have they enjoyed it. Therefore, apart from hard working, feasting, singing, dancing and celebration of different kind of festivals at various seasons were their day to day life. The sophisticated modern life in cities is self alienated. Life in cities has many problems which cannot peaceful, contended and simple life.

2. Honesty and Truthfulness

It is a twin virtue which always goes together and this is the backbone of Nagaism. The Nagas are simple man. They don't talk much. When they say something, they mean it. They do not believe in exaggeration or of tall talks. They believe in speaking the truth and doing out in action. If a Naga cannot keep his words he will lose his honor and losing honor and dignity is a shame which is worse than death. Hypocrisy, shrewdness, corruption etc. are not familiar with Nagas. They consider it as a shame and a man without a principle.

For the Nagas, lying and cheatings are taken seriously. Once a promise is given it was irrevocable. In traditional time, decision and promise are not written but mostly in words and if at once it is made it stand as it is forever. The Naga people speak truth and are honest. This is not necessarily because of fear or consciousness of what may happen but it is spontaneity which is naturally inherent in Nagas. Therefore, honesty and truthfulness are part of cultural and customary ethics which revolve around the social and political life of the Nagas.

3. Straight forwardness

It means the attitude of directness, frankness or honest approach. Nagas speak and act too bold that sometimes it breaches diplomacy. Because, the approach of diplomacy says that 'when you say yes, it means perhaps, and when you say perhaps, it means no, and when you say no, he is not a diplomat'.

For the Nagas and Nagaism, 'black is black' and 'white is white'. Black cannot be white and vice-versa. When any crime is committed, people speak out boldly and punitive actions are taken instantly without hesitation or any kind of favorism. Nagas have numerous customary laws; they have even Law of War and Law of Peace. When applying these laws, the laws are applicable to all the village-state whether big or small. There is no double standard in Nagaism. The Nagas by nature are bold and straight forward. He will speak out what he knows and what he thinks without any reservation. Sometime, Nagas are too straight forward that it hurt the sentiment of the people. When a man visits a seriously sick man, the visitor never hides his feelings or his perception. He often pours out his opinion saying, 'you are serious, you have changed completely, you may not live long, so eat and drink to your satisfaction before you die'. That is the natural Naga simple straightforwardness.

4. Generosity

Generosity is another virtue and attribute of the Nagas. Sometimes they are too generous beyond their means. Nagas being community based social set up, all their walks of life are done under the community. They work together, eat together, and stay together (Morung system), sharing together. Thus, giving or generosity is a spontaneous nature of the Nagas. They feel proud and contended when something is given to other. Sharing with neighbor, friends and relatives with whatever they have are common phenomenon. The 'Feast of Merit' is an act of generosity where the whole villagers are feasted for days. The Nagas are not selfish people. Foods are abundant. It is a great shame when someone does not have enough food to eat. Shortage of food indicates that he might have been lazy; and laziness in Nagas' society is most unwanted. Hence, Nagas are generous people ready to share with someone whatever they possess. So it is one of the noble virtues of the Nagas.

5. Helpfulness

The Nagas do not think of living in isolation. The community is interwoven in such a way that no individual can be separated. He needs society and society needs him too. Such society base social system he always need someone and someone needs him too. In a "Morung system" boys or girls dormitory system, boys and girls live in a group. This is a socializing and training ground in which different kind of training imparted by the elders to the youngster like art of singing, dancing, music, handicraft and arts of fighting with various weapons. This also acts as institution where various kind of knowledge about culture, customary law, religion, ritual and way of life are imparted. Here the elders ruled out without any reservation or hesitations are ready to help and teach them in spite of the whole day heavy work.

Even today when someone is sick, almost all the villager will visit him and help the family in cash, in kind or in service. In the Naga Society, the needy person gets immediate attention. In farming, wet paddy, terraced cultivation or jhumming cultivation, whoever finishes earlier, will definitely help the neighbor. Such humanity and helpfulness attitude is also one of the qualities of the Nagas.

6. Regards for Others

Today in the modern society, particularly in the Capitalist community where there is always competition and survival of the fittest is the trend, we hardly find people regard for other. His regards to other is mostly based on the material benefits, advantage that he would get. Therefore, it is artificial and perverted one.

In Nagas society, he finds difficult to be selfish. Elders are respected because they are the source of knowledge, records and guardian for the younger generation therefore, they are regarded. Hence a healthy feeling develops of a noble quality and everyone develop regards for others. The Naga courtesy demands thinking for other. The first person "I" or "Self" is always conditioned by others. Therefore, he learns to regard other which is greatly valued by the Nagas society.

7. Religious

One of the virtues of the traditional Nagas was that, they are very religious. Their religion is not codified; and it is not sophisticated theological doctrine and it does not have Messianic teaching. Yet, it is integral part of social life where no individuals can avoid it because social, economic and political lives are interwoven. In fact, it is a way of life. To be a Naga means, to be religious as well.

The Nagas believe in two kind of spirit:

1. The evil spirit (malevolent). They believe that evil spirit harm human being. They are everywhere. In order to avoid being harmed by it they have to perform appeasement act by offering various kind.
2. The second kind of spirit is good (benevolent) or holy one. Here too, they have many gods and the supreme god is known as "Ameowo".

Rites and ceremonies are integral part of every society. Rituals are set up, believes behavior. The Nagas have many rituals, ceremonies and rites. This beliefs system is a guiding light in Naga society.

8. Fearlessness

Nagas are brave courageous people. Every man is natural inborn warrior. This may be because, in those days head hunting was prevalent so they have to defend themselves and the whole village. The elders and warrior experts used to impart art of fighting and use of different weapon to the youngster at a very tender age. Life in those days were both 'defense and offence or you perish'. There is a saying among the Nagas that "a brave man die only once but a coward dies twice before he dies". In Naga society, in olden days a man who has not taken any head was hard to get a suitor. Head hunting was glorified in those days because it has many social, political and religious beliefs and importance. But any type of war or head hunting, it has to follow certain rules. No one dare to breach such customary law, so when it seems to be a barbaric act, they consider themselves that they are living a noble, fearless and dignified life. Without which the life of the individual will be in oblivion. Every walk of life, every season, there are full of rituals and ceremonies of the Nagas.

Nagas are not only religious but they are very superstitious too. Not a single day is passed without doing some divination or superstitious acts. For them, every phenomenon has a meaning and they tried to interpret everything in relation to their life. Some of them are:

1. Divination through egg to see in which direction the next year jhuming cultivation will be done.
2. Omenation through the chicken legs. The chicken is throttled to death and through the position of the chicken's leg predict the events.

3. Divination through a Tailor-bird chirps.
4. Divination through Bamboo splinter.
5. Divination through Dragon-fly.

These are few examples of omen and superstitious belief and practices practiced by the Nagas. This religious way of life is one of the main virtues that Nagas cannot afford to ignore it and it is one of the main pillars of Nagaism.

9. Hard Working

Nagas are predominantly farmer, cultivation are mainly in two types:

1. Paddy terrace cultivation,
2. Jhuming cultivation.

All cultivations are mostly done in community or group. While they work together, they sing and chant sweetly in unison, yelling and chanting aloud sweating profusely, yet they enjoy working it. Day in and day out, no one in the village would be seen sitting idly. They would be always engaged in one work or the other. After coming back from their farm, they will weave basket or sharpen tools or take care of their domesticated animals or chicken. They are always energetic. They never complain of too much work. Skilled and hard working people are always respected in the society. Nagas have the dignity of labor. They enjoy working in group in the rain and in sunshine. Working together in all activities is one of the binding forces of the Naga's social economic and political life. Therefore, hardworking is one of the virtues of the Nagas.

10. Rule of Law

The concept of Rule of Law is that the law should be the basis of all rules and equal justice should be assured to all.

The Nagas although their customary laws are not written; they are well maintained orally and are passed it down from generation to generation since time immemorial. The Nagas have a high sense of dignity and honor. If any man breached the customary laws or ignored it willfully, he is not respected and his dignity is at stake. Moreover, he has to be penalized for that. Secondly, the Nagas are a religious people. So they believe that when injustice are done or customary laws are not followed, the evil spirit will harm them and ill-luck be fallen on them. Therefore, they follow all their custom, culture, social and religious ceremony, ritual etc. without any prejudice. Customary laws are equally applied to everyone without any discrimination. No mercy is shown when punishment is being given for breaking the custom or breach of any norms. One of the examples is, 'incest is strictly prohibited by the Naga customary law'. If so happen, than all the villagers along with the incest couple are called up. On the appointed day, after notification and if found to be true, a pig is killed and cut into two equal half from head to tail; than the priest will expose one of the halves facing towards the sky and the other half, facing towards the ground. And he will swear in the name of god of the heaven and god of the earth not to come any harm or ill luck to the villagers and their land and not to happen again of such a shameful act. And both of them are driven towards the downward side of the river along with the slaughtered pig. In such act, no friends, relatives, etc. are expected to show any sign of sympathy. All the villagers will curse them and shooed them away from the village forever. The Nagas has various types of laws and regulations and they are followed strictly. Therefore, in Nagas' society, there is a rule of law which is also one of the back-bone of Nagaism

These ten virtues of the Nagas are unique in its own way which truly represents the divine nature of man, which I call it "Nagaism".

But as the time pass by, and the so call development and modernity sets in, things have changed. The moral value has degraded, the society is polluted and the concepts are slowly changing. Hence the Nagas are losing their identity. But as some of their unique ways of life are glaringly alive, they wanted to profess and build their identity known as Nagaism based on the above discussed virtues of the above. The above ideological assertion can be shown in the following diagram.

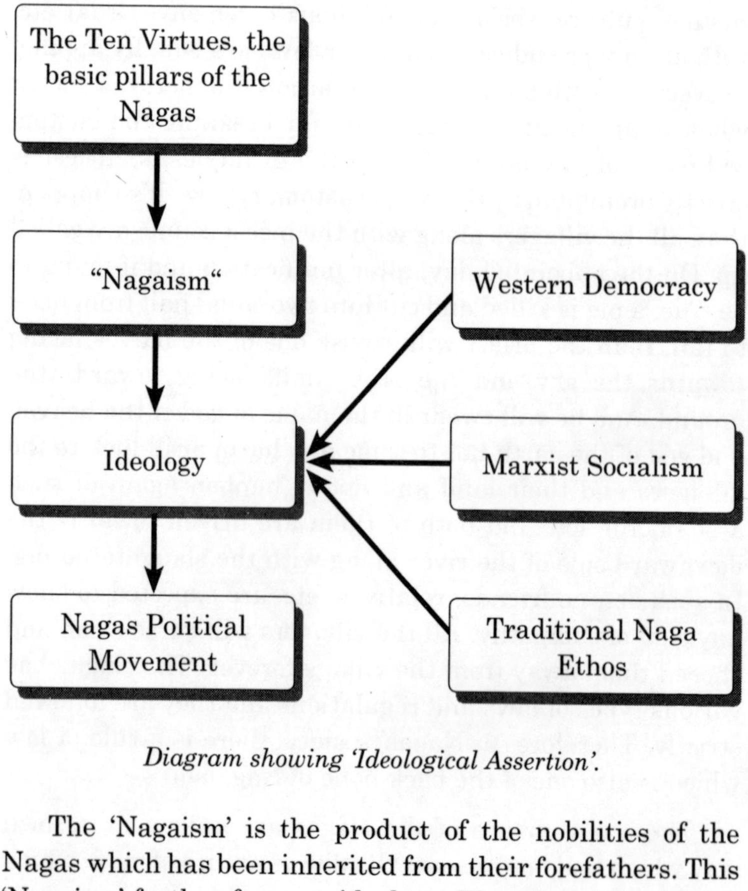

Diagram showing 'Ideological Assertion'.

The 'Nagaism' is the product of the nobilities of the Nagas which has been inherited from their forefathers. This 'Nagaism' further form an ideology. Therefore 'Nagaism' is infrastructure in which superstructure is the ideology of the Nagas is also influenced by different forces like western democracy, Marxist Socialism and Traditional Nagas ethos, which has an element of modern democracy, the rule of the wishes of the democracy and Marxist socialism which is community based economic system common holding of the means of production and sharing of the produce equally among the citizen. Therefore, this Naga ideology is the amalgamation of the different ethos of the East and the West depending on different time and circumstances. With this ideological asset with religious tone, the Nagas political movement is on since the British rule in India.

REFERENCES

1. Mark N. Hagopian, Regime Movements, and Ideologies, Longman, New York, 1970, p. 390.
2. Amal Ray and Mohit Bhattacharya, Political Theory, Ideas and Institution, The World Press Private Limited, Calcutta, p. 601.
3. Opening cited Ibid, p. 601.
4. Ideology and the Ideologists, Lewis S. Fever, Western Printing Services Ltd. Oxford-1975, p. 1.
5. Ibid. p. 2.
6. Karl Marx, The Class Struggles in France (1848-50) ed. CP. Dutt (New York). P. 114.
7. Ideology and the Ideologists, Lewis S. Fever, Western Printing Services Ltd. Oxford-1975, p. 56.
8. Op. cited: MP. Jain, Political Theory, Authors Guild Publications, Delhi, 1979, p. 612.
9. Frans Welman, Out of Isolation: Exploring a forgotten World, HPC Imprints, Green Park, Delhi, 2007, p. 27.
10. Elwin. V. Nagaland, 1961.

11. R. R. Shimray, Origin and Culture of Nagas, Delhi, 1985, p. 128.
12. Ibid., p. 129.
13. Holy Bible, King James Version, edited by Scofield, published by World Publishing U.S.A. p. 5.
14. R. R. Shimray, Origin and Culture of Nagas, Delhi, 1985, p. 253.
15. Ibid., op. cit., p. 255.

PART–II

The Genesis of the Naga Political Movement

2
Historical Background

Naga is the name of a tribe who lives mostly in the North Eastern part of India. They are of Indo-Mongoloid race speaking Tibeto-Burman language. It has about 50 sub-tribes. In spite of such vast division, there are hardly any differences in their social and cultural way of life. They are collectively known as the 'Nagas'.

After more than six decades of India's Independence the identity of the Nagas "as Indian" is still in controversy, because there are many people including the British who hold the opinion that the Nagas are not Indians. To quote one of them, "they (Nagas) are not Indian in any sense of the word neither in origin, nor in language, nor in appearance nor in habits, nor in outlook, and it is only by historical accident that they have been tacked on to an Indian province".[1] The Nagas are mostly in Nagaland, Manipur, Assam, Arunachal Pradesh and some are in upper part of Burma (Myanmar).

Sometimes the word "Nagaland" is quite confusing. Because it means a particular State, that is, Nagaland State within the Indian Union. "Nagaland can mean the lands belonging to the whole Nagas living in different States, regions, or countries. Many people loosely use this word and hence the confusion. To avoid such confusions, I prefer to use, 'Nagaland ' as the name of a particular State i.e. Nagaland state, and then the term, NAGA-LAND (Naga's land) as the whole land which comprises the whole Naga inhabited areas.

2.1. Origin of the Word, Naga

There are various opinions regarding the origin of the word Naga; but most of the views and opinions do not have a scientific basis. However, it is clear that the word "Naga "was coined by non-Nagas." This statement is supported by the following arguments:

1. No Naga would have called themselves naked as some writer opined as the origin of the word "Naga "being nakedness."
2. The word 'Naga' has no genuine or relevant meaning in the dialects of the 'Nagas'.
3. Most of the theories are based on mere speculation and imagination.
4. There is no legendary among the Naga community about the coinage of the word 'Naga'.
5. Some years back many Nagas, especially old people did not know that they were called Nagas. They were known by the names of their sub-tribes.

Thus the above points show that the word 'Naga' was coined by the outsiders or non-Nagas.

2.2. Immigration Waves

"The country now occupied by the Naga tribes was most likely subjected to mainly four immigration waves".[2] They are:

(i) The first immigration was from the direction of Tibet and Nepal which probably entered via Arunachal Pradesh (formerly known as NEFA) as some of this tribes like Noctes and Akas belong to the same Naga family.

(ii) The second immigration was the Mon-Khmer, also called Kol-Mon-Annam; these were tribes of the Indo-China Peninsula which is now inhabited by the Nagas from the south.

(iii) The third immigration probably was from the Southern China province of Yunnan across the valley of Irrawaddy, and in this movement the Tais, Shans and Ahoms formed a part. "This takes back to the first millennium of the Christian era. Groups of Thai people were moving south from or through province (now in the southern China) and beginning to established small independent kingdoms in what is now Laos, Northern Thailand, the Shan state of the present union of Burma, and the upper reaches of the Brahamaputra (Dihang) valley of Assam (India)"[3]

(iv) The fourth immigration was from the Chin Kuki group who belongs to Chin tribes of Burma. This migration was the most recent one, as late as 1918. There was migration towards Lushai Hills (now Mizoram) and the district of Churachandpur, South-West of Manipur. There are a few Kuki tribes scattered all over Naga Hills. This Chin Kuki migration was stopped by the British Government during the (1917-18) Kuki revolt.

It is believed that Kongyaks were the oldest settlers among the Nagas. Although there are many probable migration waves of the Nagas, their origin might be from the same root because they have very close affinities.

"A close examination of the implements and weapons used by the Naga tribes reveal that these very same tools are used by the Indonesian groups as well as by Igorat tribes of the Philippines".[4] Not only this, some of the social, cultural, ways of life and food habit, of the Nagas are similar to that of some people of the Asian countries. This shows that the Nagas are immigrants from those countries.

But in spite of different views, from time immemorial the Nagas always have been harboring the idea that they originate from the same root. But the geographical and climatic conditions are responsible for them to live in isolation. Moreover the economically self sufficient nature of each and every village let them to live independently. This independent nature and isolation for centuries generated hatred amongst them and they used to fight with one another. During this time there was hardly any traveler. So the people of different villages hardly knew each other. Since there was no communication or mutual exchange of ideas between the neighboring villages, they become stranger to one another. This is one of the reason that each and every village had separate dialect thou they belong to the same tribe. This further created a wide gap between them. Therefore it is obvious that since there was no sharing of feelings, thought and action and lack of concern with one another, resulting to ever ending war among the neighboring villages.

2.3. Head Hunting

Head hunting was another social practice which was highly glorified and appreciated during the early times. This act was considered as heroic. Such a glorified activity was considered as important part of social system. They believed that head hunting would bring good fortune to them and to the village. Moreover a man who hunted many heads was placed at a higher social status and was respected in the society. Even women and young children were not spared in the head hunting. In fact, killing of them was considered more velour and glorified. To quote Johnstone "To kill a baby in arms, or a women was accounted a greater feat than killing a man as it implied having penetrated to the innermost recesses of an enemy's country. Whereas man might be killed anywhere by a successful ambush".[5] Therefore, most of the time the weaker sections, like children and women were the victims. Later on, the Nagas turned from head hunting to soul hunting. It was possible through the grace of God.

The Nagas due to lack of the sense of common belongingness, did not consider themselves as one. Every village was in enmity with another village. There was no common sense of greater responsibility. So the question of the nation state did not come into their minds. Each and every village was independent, more or less like that of a Greek 'City -state. Though they imbibed this idea, the Nagas were simple and honest hill people, who could not think much about the future with the bigger national outlook. Thus, they lived in their own world of isolation.

2.4. Nagas and the Ahoms

The history of the early Nagas is not much known to us. This is because:

1. There was no written document.
2. The only history left behind was through oral from father to son and so on, and while transmitting through this process, many facts have been left out, twisted or forgotten.
3. The Nagas lived in isolation from the rest of the country. So the Indian historians' writers from abroad have very little knowledge of the Nagas. Moreover the strategic geographical condition of the North East India makes the place more isolated.

The above factors are responsible for the poor history of the Nagas. In this modem scientific age, we do not believe in legendary because they lack scientific explanation about the causation and result. But since there is no other way to fill the gap or explain the problems, we are sometimes tempted to resort to legendary, knowing its defects and unscientific explanation.

A legend says that in olden days the Tangkhul Nagas had a script which was written on animal skin. Unfortunately one day a dog carried it away and it was lost forever. This is why they don't have a script and hence there is no written document.

According to Alemchiba Ptoling, it is possibly historian only made a brief mention of the Nagas as early as the second century A.D. He located what the Hindu called Naga Log, and wrote of them as Naga Log.[6]

The meager accounts of the Hindu kings of Kamarupa from the 4th to 12th Century A.D. do not mention any connection with the Nagas. It is only through (Buranjis), the official chronicles of the Ahom kings, that they got some ideas of the Nagas history. But the Ahom kingdom started only from the thirteen century A.D.[7]

The Ahoms are mongoloid race. They were from the easternmost part of Brahamaputra valley and their language was Siamese-Chinese.

"The Ahoms entered into north Assam from Burma through the Panchore pass over the Patkai via the Nongyang Lake and through the land of Nagas of Tirap district of present Arunachal Pradesh".[8]

The first contact of Ahoms with the Nagas was violent in nature. The Nagas resisted the advancement of the Ahoms in the area inhibited by the Nagas. The Ahoms wanted the possession over salt mines in the area and to subjugate the

Nagas. So, there were many fierce fighting between the Nagas and the Ahoms. Most of the fighting took place in the Patkai Mountains.

Sukhapa, the Ahom king of Assam was reported to have compelled the Nagas to eat human flesh, the flesh of their relatives killed in the battles.[8] Such inhuman barbarous acts of Ahoms were never forgotten by the brave Nagas. The Ahom king constantly raided some of the Naga villages and some of the villages surrendered to the king. But the Nagas never gave up the fight. In these fighting the Ahoms suffered heavy casualties and lost more than that of the Nagas. The Nagas were never completely subjugated by the Ahoms. In spite of constant raids there was no domination as such by any particular tribe or ruler. It was because in those days the war was like a game of sea-sow this was because the fighting was mostly of ambush type. In such surprise attack there was every chance of winning or losing the fight. Hence, there was no subjugation or domination of the Nagas by the other. So when the Ahom tried to dominate the Nagas and took over the salt well for salt mining, the Nagas resisted to their last breath.

"The trouble with the Nagas, who lived on the low hills to Tirap close to the Plains of Sibsagar and Takhempur districts were due to economic reasons. The Ahoms had to fight the Nagas to get exclusive possession of salt wells. The salt mines were in the Naga territory and the Ahom needed them. This was another reason for continued hostility between the Ahom rulers and the Naga people of that area".[9]

In those days salt well was considered to be very precious because it was the only source of getting salt. Thus the Naga could not just let it go to the hands of the Ahoms. Moreover, the intense love of independence of the Hillman and the subjugation motives of the Ahoms were responsible for the fighting. The fighting continued for about 600 years.

"The outbreak of the Maomania rebellion, which lasted for about three decades from the last part of the 18th century appear to have altered the status quo. The rebellion in addition to bring chaos and confusion within the Ahom kingdom remained the prestige in the eyes of the hill tribes".[11] The Ahom rule in Assam came to the end before the advent of the British in Naga territory.

2.5. The Naga and the British

For thousands of years, the Nagas had remained untouched by any outside social culture and religion. But this water-tight compartment was broken by the advent of the British and the Christian missionaries in the nineteen century.

The British after assuming authority in Assam and Manipur was planning for the expansion of its authority further. India was very precious to the British; they even called India the 'Jewel of the British Grown'. So in order to keep India safe from any other rival invasion like the Burmese, it required to control the possible route to check. Since the Naga Hills is one of the possible routes, the British wanted to keep the Naga areas under its control. The British felt the necessity of annexing the Hill areas of North East India as well as the plains and valleys of the Brahmaputra and Manipur. The hill area is inhabited mainly in Assam by the people of Mongoloid tribes like Nagas, Garos, Khasis, Abhors, Meshmis, Lushais, etc. Amongst these tribes, Nagas are the most warlike tribes who used to raid frequently the Assamese and Manipuri villages.

The second reason for British annexation of the Naga areas was to protect the interest of Assam and Manipur. The king of Manipur wanted to extend his authority over the areas inhabited by the Nagas, the British also wanted to promote the interest of the king of Manipur, so that the relationship between the two could be strengthened.

Earlier, the Nagas were not united as a nation. Thus, they became easy prey of the British, but, they never gave up their fight. The British tried to be friendly with the Nagas like that of Ahoms. But when it did not materialize, the British attacked them.

In January 1832, Captain Jerking Pemberton and Gardon with 700 Manipuri troops and 800 coolies marched through Mao and Angami villages from Imphal. This was to open a suitable route between Assam and Manipur. On their way, they were attacked by the Nagas. But British with the Manipuri troops passed through and whatever they encountered on their way, they attacked. They also burnt many houses and left behind enormous destructions; many were killed and the properties of the Nagas were severely damaged.

The Manipur king, Gambhir Singh took active interest in this expedition because the Nagas posed a potential threat to his kingdom. The joint venture of the Manipur king and the British was successful in occupying some of the Nagas' territories. These areas were kept under the control of the Manipur king under certain terms and conditions. The king had to help the British whenever the later needed his help. "Thus the control of the western Nagas had also fallen in the hands of Manipur. However, Manipur afterwards sank into the British background and no longer dreamt of exerting its supremacy upon the Nagas which it had finally wielded".[12]

The British, in order to make their position safe entrusted the control of the hostile Nagas into the hands of Manipur and Cachar. "In 1935 the border between Manipur and Assam was fixed at the forest between the Doyang rivers".[13]

But the Nagas did not recognize the arbitrary demarcation which was in the interest of Manipur, Cachar, Assam and the British. Therefore, there was continuous attack by the Nagas.

In 1850 the British attitude towards the Nagas had changed due to direct contact of the Nagas by the British.

Secondly, the Anglo-Burmese war of 1834 and the Sepoy Mutiny of 1857 were also responsible for changing the British attitude toward the Nagas. Thus, the British per sued a policy of non-interference towards the Nagas. This policy had resulted in better understanding between the two. But in 1854 the relation took a different direction. This was when the Manipuri forces attacked the Angami village. About 22 villages requested the British Government to protect them. But the British Government refused to do so, on the ground that this area was not considered to be a part of the British authority and so the Nagas could not be protected.

The main interest of the British for colonial expansion was for economic gain. Therefore, the British did not take much interest in the affairs of the Nagas. The only interest was the strategic location of the areas inhabited by the Nagas.

Sir Robert Reid in his book *History of the Frontier Areas bordering of Assam (From 1883-1941)* wrote thus: "The final decision to make the Nagas Hills a British district was taken in 1881..."[14]

Such a decision was rather late because the British had always invaded the Nagas in 1832. This explains why the British regarded the strategic geographical location of the Naga areas to be more important than any other.

The British policy towards the Nagas was more of reformation and development than exploitation, when MC

Cabe, the Deputy Commissioner (1881-1894), of the Nagas Hills was appointed, he was advised to have friendly and cordial relations with the Nagas and solve any problem through peaceful means.

Under the British, the headman was given the supreme authority for the administration of the Nagas village. He had the power of deciding the disputes, both of civil and criminal nature according to customary law. The British also introduced western education. It was later assisted by the Christian missionaries. In short the "Anglo-Naga affairs may be divided into three broad periods. I. Period of exploration, II. Period of expedition, III. Period of control".[15]

I. The period of exploration

This was in the early period when the British did not have much idea and contact with the Nagas. "The first ever British team to visit the Naga Hills was led by Captain Jerkins and Penberton".[16]

This was in January 1832. When the team consisting of 700 coolies passed through the Nagas territories to establish a link between Assam and Manipur. In this exploration, they were fiercely attacked by the Nagas.

II. The period of expedition

This started from late 1830s. In January 1839 the British under the command of Sub-assistant, Grange came to the Nagas country to carry out British expedition to the Naga Hill. He was not much successful because of the Naga resistance. However, in the second expedition, he reached an agreement with the Nagas who agreed to pay annual tributes to the British. But in April 1844 when Grange's assistant went to collect the 1st year's tribute, the Nagas refused to pay and fighting took place.

During 1850-51 there was about 10 expeditions and was later on followed by a treaty of non-interference. This lasted for about 15 years.

III. The period of control

First the British were not able to control the Naga areas. From 1854-1865 there were as many as 19 raids committed by the Nagas resulting in the loss of 232 British subjects including some officers. The British therefore lost their interest in the Nagas because of the losses and sufferings. So they introduced a policy of non-interference. The areas inhabited by the Nagas were kept under the indirect control and also passed the inner line regulation of 1873 was passed. This inner line regulation was passed for the following reasons.

1. During the period of 1860–1873, there was rapid tea cultivation along the frontier of the Naga Hills. The British occupied the whole of Assam and claimed control over Burma. The administration of the Naga Hills was separated from Assam, for the convenience of administrative purpose. This cultivation led to friction between the tea planters and the Nagas. This had resulted into the passing of inner line regulation.
2. The British realized that the 'Naga' is a distinct race, socially, culturally and politically from the people of the plains. Therefore, the British wanted to protect the identity of the Nagas.
3. The Nagas were fierce warriors. To avoid confrontation with other people, the inner line regulation was passed.

2.6. The Naga between the two World Wars

The First World War did not much affect the Nagas except for the labor corps sent to France. About 2000 Nagas were sent to France to participate in the First World War. There, the Nagas started to know the outside world with their own experience.

But the Second World War affected the Nagas to a great extent. Many battles were fought in the Naga Hills. The fiercest battle was fought in Kohima between the Japanese and the Allied soldiers. Many officers of both allied and Japanese praised the Naga's hospitality, bravery and honesty. The Nagas for the first time saw with their eyes the world in flames.

The British control of the Naga Hills came to an end when India got independence in 1947.

REFERENCES

1. Maxwell Neville. Indian the Nagas and the North East MRG Report No 17, London Revised edition 1980, p. 3.
2. Horam M. Naga Insurgency, Cosmo Publication, New Delhi, 1988, p. 5.
3. South East Asia (ed) Alice Taylor 1972, p. 83.
4. Dr. M. Horam op. cit.
5. James Johnstone, Manipur and the Naga Tribe, Minas Publication, Delhi, 1987, p. 30.
6. Alemchiba, A brief Historical Account of Nagaland, Naga Institute of Culture,Kohima, 1970, p 22.
7. Murkot Rammuny, The world of Nagas Northern Book Centre. New Delhi, 1988, p. 10.
8. Ibid. p. 10.
9. Roland Shimmi, Oppenion cited. Comparative History of the Nagas, Inter-India publication Delhi, 1988, p. 146.
10. M. Rammuny. The World of Nagas, Northern Book Century, New Delhi, 1988, p. 1.
11. Ibid. p. 12.

12. Asoso yonuo, The Rising Nagas, Vivek Publication House, Delhi, 1974, p. 75.
13. Ibid., p. 75.
14. Reid Robert, History of the frontier areas Bordering on Assam front 1883- 1941 (Extract from) The Rising Nagas, Asoso Yonuo. Vivik Publishing House Delhi 1974, p. 107.
15. M. Horam. Naga Polity. B.R Publication corporation Delhi 1975, p. 9.
16. Mills a S Moifatt, Report on the province of Assam 1854. Pp. cxlv-clxii.

3

Causes of the Naga Political Movement

The following are some of the factors responsible for the causes of the Naga political movement.

3.1. Nationalism

"Nationalism is the political belief that some group of people represents a natural community which should live under one political system be independent of others, and often has the right to demand and equal standing in the world order with other".[1]

The term 'Nation State' is a modern phenomenon. But nationalism, the love of one country in the traditional sense can be traced back to ancient times. But it was the impact of science and technology which made 'Nationalism' to grow stronger and deeper.

Common language, religion or some genetic poll are some of the factors for the growth of Nationalism. But more important factor is the element of will, a will to form together. Will is the desire of the people to form a Nation.

3.2 Naga Nationalism

Naga Nationalism is a modern phenomenon. However the seed was sown during the time of British rule. And it came into being with a stronger force after India Independence. Naga nationalism has been viewed from different angles. Some are of the opinion that "Naga Nationalist sentiment is based on the fact that the Nagas are different from the Indians".[2] Some desire to call the Naga political movement indulging in guerilla activities as 'Naga Nationalism'. There are others who want to call it 'semi-nationalism' or sub-nationalism.

3.3. Social Factor

The social structure of the Naga is quite different from that of the other people of India. It was mainly for this reason that the British classified the Naga areas as Excluded area in 1935.

The Nagas were independent and self sufficient in the past days. Each and every village was more or less independent like that of the "Greek - City state". Socially man and woman are treated equally. There is no discrimination on the basis of caste, creed, sex or color. Everyone is equal before the eyes of the customary law and before the society; every individual enjoys and gets his or her share according to what it should be. Peoples, in earlier times were brave, sometimes barbarous but honest. There was no slave or master, no rich or poor. This paradise-like-society was disturbed by the coming of the British. This past glory of the Naga society has drifted away slowly from the Nagas and is replaced by a new society which is neither indigenous nor western or Indian. This synthesis is reacted by the young generation of the Nagas who want to trace their original culture and their heritage.

Secondly, the educated Nagas want to trace their original past history. This in turn resulted in the emergence of the spirit of nationalism in their minds. This is the most important factor that gives rise to Naga Nationalism.

3.4. Fear Psychosis

The Nagas have developed a fear psychosis, the reasons are: first, the Nagas are small communities compared to the rest of the Indians. So there is a fear of domination over this minority by the majority Hindus. Secondly, the Nagas are Hill tribes. They were considered by the mainland Indians as savage and uncivilized. They visualize that they will be treated as an inferior race, if merged together.

Thirdly, the Indian society is divided into social classes such as, rich and poor. The poor has no say in the society. This is new to the Nagas. The Nagas fear that if they are merged with India, they will turn into lower social class citizens.

But the most psychosis fear of the Nagas is caste system, dividing the society into strict hierarchical form.

It is believed among the Hindu that the four Varnas came into being from the body of the primeval man. From his mouth issued the Brahmins, who became priests and scholars. From his arms came the Kshetriyas, warriors and rulers; from his thighs came the Vaishyasm tradesman, and from his feet rose the Sudras, cultivators'.[3] This segregation is permanent and is determined by birth. The people of the three higher caste i.e. Brahmins, Kshetriyas, and Vaishyas are considered to be pure and 'twice born' caste. But Sudra is considered to be impure and is in the lowest rung of the society.

The Indians placed Hillman like the Nagas in the lowest rung of the society. The Nagas strongly oppose against such segregation. They believe that if integrated with the rest of Indians they will be placed in the lowest rung and hence they would be subjected to exploitation and humiliation, visualizing this probability, the Nagas do not like to be integrated with the rest of the Indians, specially, the Hindus.

Lastly, the Nagas glorified their society and their social integration, specially the Morung[4] system. The social interaction mainly takes place in the Morung. The Naga felt that if they are integrated in the Hindu cultural lives, their social system will be dominated and suppressed by the Social system of the majority.

3.5. Economic Factor

Every Naga village was self sufficient economically. Every village produced its essential things. However in course of time, the Nagas are more and more alienated from themselves. The advancement of modern science and technology disintegrated their society. The modern machines enslaved them. The Nagas lost their original individuals skill and energy. Moreover, with the integration into the Indian Union, some Indian businessman took advantage of the Naga's ignorance and honesty. This slowly swept away the wealth of the Nagas.

"God given natural resources are now turning barren. The rich forest is almost barren, living creatures in the rivers are almost disappearing. All four footed animals in the jungles have vanished. All birds are being killed"'.[5] This is how Rev. V. K. Nuh has expressed the condition of the Nagaland after India's Independence. The Nagas who are hard working people in the past have now turned into lazy and leisure living people. There is rampant corruption. The central government is granting huge amount of money to the Nagaland State. Large amount of money is often misused and not utilized for development. It thus directly spoils the Nagas. As a result of this, the outsiders take advantage of the economic situation.

The worst affect of the Nagas was Economics advantage taken by the outsiders and hence exploitation. Rev. V K. Nuh has pointed out the following 5 points.[6]

1. 75% commerce is in the hands of outsiders.
2. 75% leaders are in the hands of outsiders.
3. 75% leaders are purchased by Marwaris.
4. 75% Naga public quotas are in the hands of outsiders.
5. 75% plan or non-plan budget has commodities purchased from outsiders.
6. 75% publicity and mass media communication are influenced by outsiders.
7. 75% education personals are outsiders.

Apart from this, today, in any Naga metropolitan cities or towns, the biggest business shop is owned or run by the non- Nagas. Thus economically, the Nagas are dependent on the non-Nagas. This made the Nagas strangers in their own land. This has resulted in creating political consciousness among the educated Nagas to liberate themselves from this economic bondage, thus giving rise to the feeling of nationalism.

3.6. Religious Impact

The conversion of the Nagas into Christianity was greatest revolution in the Naga history, which is more significant and important than British colonialism. The British hardly received any economic benefits from the Nagas as they were not rich enough. But a small amount of taxes were collected from some villages, but this was not enough to maintain the administration. Moreover, the frequent raids and the resistance of the Nagas against the British had diverted their interest. Hence they followed the policy of non-interference and non-interaction.

The Missionaries were very much attracted towards the social practices and customs of the Nagas, specially head hunting, etc.

The first group of American missionaries, Baptist missionaries made their appearance in the Naga areas in the 1830s. But before they came to the Naga areas they had heard that the Nagas were "Head hunters". This, the missionaries found to be true.

Tusom village situated in the Manipur East District, bordering Nagaland and Burma, a man called Mr. Z. Khaisang and his brother Z. Lukhoi, along with H. Phungpho, H. Kuisang and other friends were converted to Christianity. As they were not allowed to settle together in their old village they decided to move out and settle nearby. Accordingly H. Phungpho first moved out and settled in the new found village. Subsequently the rest followed him within few days. Consequently they were excommunicated by the villagers. The new settled village is about two K.m. away from their original village and they named the village as "Tusom Christian Village". Still they were not set free. They were asked to follow non - Christian norms, rituals, rules and regulations of the heathen (non-Christian) society. As they had been converted into Christianity they did not observe them. Therefore, they were heavily fined. One may note that in those days conversion into Christianity was not easy one. Of course the taste was bitter but God's rewarding result was sweet. A man who was converted into Christianity was the first to get education. "The missionaries and the more specific the protestant missionaries often exalted the Bible as the ultimate source of authority and made it a condition that if an individual had not work God aright, he must be able to read."[7] So Christianity goes hand in hand with education.

The missionaries felt that without education it would not be possible to convert or spread Christianity. Good and better Christians need to know how to read Bible and sing song. And one must be self sufficient or self reliant politically and economically. In order to be economically self sufficient, the reformations were made:

1. Weaving, including all process in the preparation of cotton from seed and dyeing,
2. Needle works including simple cutting out,
3. Basket works in Bamboo and Cane,
4. Simple pottery, using local clay,
5. Baby welfare, infant care, first aid and home nursing including cooking,
6. Knitting and crochet work with home to grow cotton, and bamboo for the girls,
7. Gardening, including experiments with seeds and plants,
8. Farm work including:
   (a) care arid breeding of cows, goats, pigs, fowls, pigeons, ducks, etc.,
   (b) the milking of cows and wild goats,
   (c) making of creams and butter with such implements which could be secured and used in any village,
9. Household managements including cooking and laundry work,
10. Clay modeling, including maps,
11. Other handiworks including drawing, painting, crayon work and inset fitting etc.,

12. Singing and Tonic Sol-fa,

13. Dramatization,

14. Drill games and simple dances.'[8]

The missionaries were able to experiment successfully in all these fields. For the Nagas, Christianity was the root of development. It acted as the main training ground for leadership and vital influencing factor for social, economic and political consciousness and development of the people.

It was the missionaries, through education, produced leaders which brought about political consciousness.

It cannot be denied that Christianity and western education brought the emerging modern elites with liberal ideas which inspired the political movement especially in North-East India. But it will be wrong to say that missionaries or Christianity was the direct cause of the Nagas political movements. It is only one of the influencing factors for the Naga political movements.

3.7. Political Consciousness

No man can live outside the society. He needs society and the society needs him too. Man is therefore social being by nature. Man acts with rational thought, but animals act with instinct. But rationality and consciousness of man is not always constant and equal. The environmental factors, specially socio-economic and political advancement and condition very much influenced one's level of consciousness. Therefore, though rationality and consciousness is inborn in man, the pace of development depends on the environment and condition which surrounds him.

Before the advent of the British, the Nagas were unknown to the rest of the world. The modern sense of

Nation state or Independence was not known to them, but every Naga Village had been a republic having its own village Government and each village being socially self sufficient.[9]

However much was changed with the advent of the British. The American Baptist missionaries spread Christianity imparting education and other western culture. It was through this education that the Nagas opened a new chapter of their social and political life.

It was in August 1914 that the world witnessed the beginning of one of the most terrible and destructive wars in the history of mankind which was generally known as the First World War. It was by sheer luck that some of the Nagas stepped out to the outside world. About 2000 Nagas were recruited as Labor corps and went to France. They were fascinated by the world around them and they came back much enlightened. When they returned, their interest moved towards the western education and culture. Hence, they encouraged their children and friends to pursue western system of education.

Slowly and steadily, western education and culture penetrated into the life of the Nagas. Christianity spread like wild fire in the Naga areas. It is through Christianization that schools and other institutions sprang up in every nook and corner, making the people more conscious of the western culture.

Meanwhile, World War II broke out, and reached Indian soil in the early 1940s. One of the bloodiest battles was fought in Kohima. This fighting between the Allies and the Axis power in the Naga area for almost six months had made a great impact on the Nagas.

This was the first time in the history of the Nagas that extreme society of East and West met together, personally in groups. This alien social culture influenced the Nagas in many ways including well organized political and hierarchical form of activities and strict adherence to law and order and well discipline, are some of the things which surprised the Nagas. As the saying goes "Seeing is believing", the foreigners' activities before their eyes left great impact in minds of the Nagas. "The Naga had seen a modem war. They had watched the Japanese and allies fighting in the jungles. Unknowingly they had trained themselves for jungles warfare. From ancient days Nagas were fighters. But their weapons were spears and daos. The jungle was the background for all warfare they knew for defence as well as attack. But the Second World War brought them into a new warfare".[10]

Apart from the influences two great world war, there are others which are more effective for the growth of the political consciousness of the Nagas. They are the different organizations, clubs, and unions etc. The first of this kind was the Naga Club formed in 1918.

3.8. Naga Club

The Labor corps which went to France in the First World War came back with new ideas. They along with the educated Nagas organized themselves and formed the Naga Club in 1918. The chief concern of this organization was the political future of the Nagas. This was the turning point in the history of the political movement of the Nagas. To quote N.K. Das in his article "The Nagas movement", "The origin of the present Nagas movement could be traced first to the formation of Nagas Club in the year 1918 at Kohima with a branch at Mokokchung."[11]

The members of the organization were modern bureaucrats, emerging elites and some of the leaders in the villages. They mainly discussed the social and the administrative problems of the Nagas. It first submitted a memorandum to the Simon Commission in 1929. In the memorandum, the Nagas expressed their ideas, desires and feelings and anxieties of the people. The main theme of this memorandum was a prayer for keeping the Hills outside the Scheme of reforms and to keep the Naga Hills under the direct British administration.

This memorandum also mentioned many other economic issues. They are:

1. The memorandum pointed out that the education of the Nagas was poor and their population was small, and subsequently the representation allotted to them in the council of a bigger province (Assam) would be negligible.
2. The memorandum also said that the Naga languages were quite different from those of the plain people and they have had no social affinities with the Indian, either Hindus or Muslims.
3. The Nagas felt they have been looked down upon, for eating beef and pork,
4. It was feared that new taxes would be imposed upon them, and they might not have any share in their forest and lands. They said that the British Government had always recognized the Naga right over their hills. Under the new arrangements they might lose their rights over their hills. So they might be kept beyond the ambit of the proposed reforms and placed directly under the British Government.
5. The Naga leaders expressed their apprehension of the 'Introduction' of foreign laws and customs to supersede our own customary laws', and desired to be left alone 'to determine for ourselves as in ancient times".[12]

The Nagas felt that the British had sympathy for the Nagas. They felt that if the British suddenly left India, the Nagas would be under the mercy of the Indian Government.

In course of time the political consciousness of the Nagas was raised. Many organizations, unions and Councils at various levels were formed. The Lotha Council was formed in 1923 and Ao Council by 1928 and many more Councils were established by the middle of the forties.

The next landmark in the historical background of the Nagas movement was the formation in April 1945 of the Naga Hills District Tribal Council, uniting the individual tribal council under the initiative of the then Deputy Commissioner of the Naga Hills District.[13] The name of this council was changed into Naga National Council in 1946.

REFERENCES

1. David Robertson Dictionary of Politics, Penquin Publication, London 1985, p. 225.
2. M. Horam, Naga Insurgency, Cosmo publication, Delhi, 1988. p. 34.
3. Bashan A.L. The wonder that was India. London 1954, pp. 240-241.
4. Morung is a dormitory where bachelor youth came together and social activities take place.
5. Rev. V.K. Nuh. My Country...... p. 45.
6. Rev. V.K. Nuh. My country my people published by Chakhesang Student Union, 1988, p. 47.
7. Lord M.A. Missionary and Education in Bengal 1793-1837. Oxford, pp. 3-4.
8. An Educational Experience, 1920-1930, Baptist Mission South Lushai girls School, p. 2.

9. K.S. Singh, Tribal movement in India, Vol. 1. Manohar Publication New Delhi 1982, p. 41.

10. Murkot Rammuny. The world of Nagas, Northern Book Centre. Delhi, 1988, p. 29.

11. K.S. Singh. The Tribal Movements in India. Vol 1 Manohar publication, Delhi, p. 29.

12. Ibid., pp. 42-43.

13. K.S. Singh. op. cit., p. 43.

4

Movements: Naga National Council

It is difficult to locate the exact time and place of the beginning of the Naga National movement. However it will not be wrong to say that the formation of the Naga Club in 1918 was the beginning of the Naga National movement. Prior to this, there were fighting between the Nagas and the Ahoms, and then the Nagas and the British which created a sense of security and integrity among the Nagas. But there was no public forum or organization to express their views. Thus to meet the urgent need of an organization, the educated youth founded the Naga Club in 1918 at kohima. This was the turning point of the Nagas. In this club, almost all topics ranging from social to political problems were discussed. This was the first organization where different tribes, came together to discuss their future.

Some of the Naga leaders visualized that very soon the British would leave India and soon the Nagas political problems would arise. Seeing this, the Naga leaders persuaded the British not to link up the Nagas with the rest of Indians.

The Naga Hills District which was under the Lt. Governor of Bengal was, in 1874, a part of the province of

Assam. Its administration was regulated by a number of acts which made special provisions for undeveloped tracts.

The Government of India act of 1919 permitted the Governor General to declare any Territory in India to be backward tract'.[1]

When Simon Commission visited the Naga Hills to find out the wishes of the Nagas about the political future, the Nagas submitted a Memorandum saying: "It is the purpose of this note to show that the interest of hill districts will not be served by having them included in the reforms but they will suffer very serious determent by being tied up to the politically more advanced plains district, while the later are likely to suffer in the future by being joined with people of irreconcilable culture is an unnatural union which can ultimately only entail discomfort for both party.[2]

Here Hutton being an anthropologist and having been associated with the Naga people for about twenty years or so, he has seen clearly that the Nagas and the rest Indian culture are quite different from one another therefore he feels that it will be unwise to unite. Because, it will be an unnatural union. Hence he objected any step to unite the Nagas with the rest of India or categorized them together with others.

This observation made by a foreigner deeply influenced the Nagas.

4.1 The Simon Commission

On January 10, 1929 a Commission led by Sir John Simon with Mr. Attlee as one of the members visited Kohima to find out the wishes of the Nagas about their political future. The leaders under the banner of Naga Club submitted a memorandum. The following points are some of contents of the memorandum, that (1) the Nagas regretted to learn it would be included in the reformed scheme. They requested not to do so as the Nagas do not ask for reforms and they do not wish for any reforms.

Before the British conquered the Naga Hills in 1879-80, they had constant warfare with Assamese and Manipuris. But none of them conquered it. The Naga's social and cultural system is quite different from that of others including the people of neighboring areas. The memorandum said that 'Our education is very poor and population is comparatively very small, we are looked down by the Hindus and the Muslims for eating of beef and pork that our country is poor. Therefore, we cannot bear new heavy taxes and we are afraid of domination by the majority tribe. Moreover, we have the fear for the introduction of foreign laws and customs to supersede our own customary laws which we now enjoy. For the above said reasons the Nagas would not like to be in the reformed scheme'."[3]

From this memorandum we see that the Naga people were afraid of exploitation, racially, economically and politically.

In May 1935 reports of the Commission were placed before the special committee on Indian bill before the House of Commons in London, the issue was taken up in the midst of Contradictory reports as some members of the House called the Nagas "backwards" and the meeting as "nauseating". Mr. Cadogan called this reports "misleading". He further argued that because the Naga customs differed from British customs did not mean or prove that the Nagas were "backward" in any sense'.[4]

Mr. Cadogan was one of the honorable members of the British Parliament who had visited the Naga Hills and had seen the Nagas and was convinced that they were more sophisticated in their own ways than what the British man think of them. "The Nagas", he said, "had a very shrewd suspicion that something is being done to away from their immemorial right and custom".[5] The British realized that all the tribal areas in India needed a special kind of administration for their simple and unsophisticated nature.

The Government of India Act 1919 empowered the Governor General to proclaim any part of India to be "backward area". But the word backward was strongly objected. So it was decided to call this category as "Excluded Area" in April 1937, The Naga Hills District along with North Eastern Frontier Tract, the Lushai hills and Cachar Hills were declared "Excluded Hills" of the province of Assam.

4.2 Naga National Council (NNC)

Just after the end of the Second World War, with the help of the British Deputy Commissioner of the Naga Hills, an institution called "Naga Hills District Tribal Council" was formed in 1945. This was to unite the whole Naga areas on the modern administrative lines. The following year in March 1946 a meeting at Wokha passed a resolution changing the name of the council into *Naga National Council.* In this council different Naga tribes were represented through a system of proportionate representation.

There are similarities between the formation of the Indian National Congress in 1885 and the Naga National Council. Both the organizations were the first ever formed to unite the masses on the modern lines. Both the organizations were started with the initiative of non local person on the liberal way. Later on, these organizations became the Flag bearer of the Independent movements. Both organizations unified the masses. Like that of the Indian national Congress, the moderate leaders the early stage had faith in the British and believed that, only the British could bring development to the undeveloped Indians and Nagas. But there were few sections of people in the Congress during the early 20th century who no longer had faith and did not want to associate with the British. Likewise, the Naga National Council, on the eve of Indian independence was not consensus. Some Nagas demanded immediate independence, others were not in favor of complete break away from India, and yet there were people who were inclined to remain as British Mandatory state. But the majority favored the first one. So the NNC under the leadership of Phizo declared Naga's Independence on August 14, 1947. The NNC in this period adopted the decision that the "British must go" and the central Government of India should act as the guardian power for a period of ten years after which the Naga would decide their future. In the meanwhile the Government of India set up a Committee of the Aboriginal tribes. The sub-committee of the advisory committee had to visit Kohima to find out the wishes of the Nagas. In the welcome address to the sub-committee members on may 20, 1947 T. Sakhrie, the then General Secretary of NNC said "you have come to find out from us the desire of the Naga people on the question of how their land should be governed when the British power withdraws from India. I am sure that members of the Naga National Council who are all present in this house will make your task easy that Nagas are indivisible and have one voice. I hope you will do all in your power to help the Nagas achieve their demand".[6]

The NNC put forward the following terms to be conveyed to the Government of India

1. The interim Government of Naga people will rule over all the people of Nagaland having full power in respect of Legislation, Executive and Judiciary.
2. Nagaland belongs to the Naga people and will be inalienable.

3. The Interim Government of the Naga people will have full power in the matters of raising revenue and expenditure an annual subvention to cover the deficit given by the Guardian power.[7]

With these terms and conditions to the Government of India, the Naga political movement moves ahead in full swing under the leadership of Phizo.

4.3 Zapu Phizo

Zapu Phizo was an Angami who was born in about 1900 A.D. at Kohima. Due to his financial problems, he did not have a proper education during his childhood days. He was not successful in business too. Although he did not have higher education he was a man who possessed a quality of leadership. He also had a charismatic personality. Through his leadership, the Nagas who lived in isolation wedded with tribalism and tribal rivalry were united under one roof with the help of NNC organization. Mahatma Gandhi was the leader of India who brought the different sections of people and united them and made the Indian National Movement a mass movement. The same could be said of Phizo. Phizo was a leader who unified the different tribes of the Nagas and made Naga movement a mass movement. In fact, Phizo came at the right time and in the right place where the Nagas needed a dynamic leadership.

When World War II broke out in 1939, the future of the Nagas seemed to be bleak. The Indian National Movement under the leadership of Nehru and Mahatma Gandhi took advantage of the war. The Nagas, on the other hand, due to lack of a good leader and ignorance of the masses could not take advantage of the situation.

The allied forces entered the Indian soil via Burma passing through the Naga areas. Since the fighting was on constantly for many months, the Naga villagers could not go to their paddy fields. Hence the village economy was badly affected.

Phizo went to Rangoon via Calcutta with his family and his brother Keviyally due to constant allied bombing, Phizo with his family had to move to Taikkya and it was during the 1st week of December, 1943 that he had an attack of facial paralysis and erysipelas.[8]

A report says that in 1943 he had joined the INA and was with them till 1945. After recapture in Burma he was detained along with other INA personnel by the British.

In 1945 while he was in Burma he heard that Kohima had been liberated by Netaji (S.Bose). He wrote a letter to Netaji Subhas Chandra Bose congratulating him and wished him further success in his drive towards India and against British imperialism. He requested Netaji to arrange transport facilities for himself and family so that he could come to Kohima to help him liberate India with the help of the Nagas.

Phizo after release from detention in Rangoon returned to Kohima along with his family. When he reached home, he was actively involved in NNC activities. He visited different places of the Naga inhabited areas and lectured for the liberation of the Nagas. It is said that, he even used to carry sweets in his pocket and distributed to the women and children, to draw attention and win their love and affection after that he lectured and taught them about nationalism. He was also very much concerned about the upliftment of the Nagas. Phizo disagreed moderate policies and formed the people's Independence League in May 1947 to launch movement for full independence. On account of his anti-national activities he was arrested and imprisoned in 1949. However he was released later on compensatory grounds following his son's death in a motor accident.

In 1951 a Naga delegate led by Phizo went to Delhi to meet the Prime Minister of India to discuss about the Naga political aspiration. The Prime Minister, Nehru was not positive towards their demand. This gave more inspiration to Phizo and his colleagues. They came back and prepared to further the campaign for Nagas Independence. They collected signatures and thumb impressions from the people and appealed to all the Nagas to rise to work for freedom. All the Nagas responded with enthusiasm and about 99% of the people supported the struggle for independence. In March 1952 Phizo presented the result of the plebiscite to the President of the Congress. And another meeting was arranged with Nehru. But he completely turned down the Naga demand. It is said that Nehru lost his temper and said, if the heaven falls and India went to pieces the Nagas would not be given Independence. Zapu Phizo with his colleagues once again came back empty handed. Thus there was no way out except resorting to violence. Hence the Naga national Movement took an armed struggle with India. Today, after Phizo's death, he has become one of the most controversial leaders in the history of the Naga Political movement. Most of the Nagas criticized him for staying away in London for a long time. He was also criticized for being silent in the so called "Shillong Accord". In spite of all these criticisms, it may be said that Phizo was the person who has contributed much to the Naga National movement. Undoubtedly he is the father of Naga National political movement.

4.4 Crux of the Political Problem

Immediately after the visit of the Advisory Committee of the Constituent Assembly, Sir Akbar Hydary, the then Governor of Assam visited Kohima on June 27- 28, 1947 and had long discussions with the NNC. After a long series of discussion, the meeting arrived at an agreement which is popularly known as the "Nine Points Agreement".[9] In this agreement, the right of the Nagas to develop themselves according to their wishes was recognized. Article 9 of the agreement was the most controversial one. It reads as follows, Article 9, *Period of Agreement:* "The Governor of Assam as the agent of the Government of the Indian Union will have a special responsibility for a period of 10 years to insure the due observance of this agreement; at the end of this period the Naga Council will be asked whether they required the above Agreement to be extended for a further period of a new agreement regarding the future of the Naga people arrived at."[10]

It is a fact that this article is vaguely worded. It can be interpreted in many ways. The Nagas interpreted this article to mean that they had the right to claim independence after a period of 10 years. To the Indian Government, it means that after 10 years the same agreement may be renewed or a fresh agreement may be arrived at. The interpretation of the same article in different angles formed the crux of the Naga problem. After the conclusion of the agreement, controversies started between the Nagas and the Indian Government. Unfortunately, in the midst of this confusion, Sir Hydary expired. But the Naga leaders believed that they have reasons according to article 9 of the agreement. Because this agreement was concluded at the time when the Naga problem was on and the meeting was held in connection with Naga's independence they regarded that article 9 of the agreement will lead them to self-determination and independent.

To clarify the opinion and the position of the Nagas the NNC session was held at Kohima on December 11, 1950. A resolution was passed to hold a plebiscite on the issue of Naga Independence.

According to a circular letter dated 30th April, 1951 addressed to all the President of Tribal's Councils, Phizo stated "Every person must feel perfectly free to say and record what he or she likes. We are fighting for Independence, for fuller freedom, for a separate sovereign state of Nagaland. But for those people if there is any wish to say that Nagaland must be within the Indian Union they must have the full freedom to express their view without fear. I hope everyone will have the courage to say exactly what he or she wants to say".[11]

Plebiscite was held and the result indicated that about 99% of the Nagas in the Naga Hills District were in support of the demand for independence. This result was sent to the President of the Indian Republic and other important personalities but no one gave heed to it. Hence it added more fuel to the Naga's burning problem.

As time went by the Naga political problem became more serious. The Nagas boycotted the first general election of India held in 1952 under the direction of the Naga National Council. No one filed nomination for candidature. No one turned up to cast vote. On the other hand, the Naga National Council was strengthened and more organizations emerged in order to intensify the movement.

4.5 The Underground Organization

There are mainly three bodies in the underground organization.[12]

1. The Naga National Council, a political party instituted in 1945.
2. The Federal Government of Nagaland.
3. The Federal Army.

The NNC was the only prevalent political party of the underground Nagas during this time. At first, it believed and followed nonviolence. However when the Indian Government did not pay any heed to the Naga problem, the organization took up arms in 1954. It was switched over to violence, as a means under the leadership of Phizo. He also founded the People's Independence League in 1948. This was to intensify the labors towards the Naga Independence. The NNC also played a vital role for the unification and co-operation of the Nagas as one whole. A number of voluntary groups were formed in various villages, spreading the ideology of NNC.

4.6 The Federal Government of Nagaland

Armed hostilities broke out in 1955 between the Naga Army and the Assam Rifles. Eventually, the Indian Security Force had to be called in as the underground could not be controlled by the Assam Rifles. Fighting continued intermittently. It was in 1956 that the underground ambitiously set up a Government called 'the Federal Government of Nagaland'. Its Flag was hoisted on March 22, 1956 at Phensinyu a Rengma village."[13]

A Yehzabo[14] (Constitution) was made which consists of 12 parts and 144 articles. The constitution is very short. It guarantees the well being of the people and the realization of International peace and co-operation. Regarding defense, it is laid down in parts VIII of the Yehzabo, "The Federal Government of Nagaland shall maintain a standing national army". This national army is for the protection and maintenance of law and order.

4.7 Violence

Not very long after the passing of the 9 Point Agreement, the tension between the Nagas and the Indian Government was prominently seen in the political field. In the midst of the confusion, Phizo with a few leaders met Mahatma Gandhi at 13 Bhangi Basti in New Delhi in July, 1947 to put forward the claim of the Independence. Gandhi who is the father of India replied, "We do not want the British and they are going. If you say that you are not Indians and your country does not belong to India, then the matter must end there. Nobody will force you to join the Indian Union".[15]

With this bold reply, the delegate came back with great hope, and after a few years, a plebiscite was held. The result showed that all the Nagas voted for Independence. But when this result was sent to the President of India neither the answer of the Mahatma Gandhi nor the result of the plebiscite was honored by the Indian leaders. So the Nagas boycotted the first General election. Slowly, the Naga political problem culminated into bigger problems.

Now Phizo along with some other leaders campaigned for not to pay tax to the Indian Government. "By October 1953 there were reports that some of the Naga leaders in the Naga Hills District had started asking the Gaonburas (Village Authority) not to co-operate with the Government as they were paid by the villagers and not by the Government".[16] Meanwhile, the Indian Government took up various developmental programs like the establishment of Schools and other allied program to win the heart of the Nagas.

But the seed of contradiction had already been sown creating tension in almost all parts of the Naga areas which was beyond control of any leader. Hence from every nook and corner, report of violence between the Nagas and the Indian soldiers was heard. As a result by 1954 little spark of fire was just enough to ignite a bigger flame. Since then there has been no rest and peace in all over the Naga inhabited areas.

REFERENCES

1. Murkot Rammuny. The world of Naga. Northern Book centre, New Delhi 1988, p. 23.
2. Ibid., p. 23.
3. Opinion cited from a Memorandum Submitted by the Nagas to Simon Commission.
4. M. Horam. Naga Insurgency, Cosmo Publication, New Delhi, 1988, p. 40.
5. Ibid., p. 40.
6. M. Horam. op. cit., p. 42.
7. Ibid., p. 42.
8. M. Ramunny op. cit., p. 53.
9. Refer full text.
10. Article 9. Nine point agreement.
11. M. Ramunny op. cit., p. 57.
12. M. Horam op. cit., p. 58.
13. Ibid., p. 59.
14. The constitution of the Federal Government of Nagaland having 131 articles.
15. A Souvenir published by Literature committee. Naga 90 Gauwahati-21. 1990, p. 11.
16. M. Rammuny. The world of Nagas, Northern Book Centre New Delhi, 1988, p. 70.

5

Agreements; Accord and Their Impact

The Naga political journey is a lengthy one, characterized by ups and down. Many steps have been taken up to solve the problem. Many agreements and accords were signed. However complete peace is still out of sight. The main reason for the failure of any agreement or accord is lack of consensus.

The followings are some of the factors responsible for the failure of the agreement or accord:

1. The Nagas by nature, from time immemorial have a feeling of individual liberty. They value individual freedom more than unity as a whole.
2. The Nagas comprised of many Sub-tribes; each tribe has certain differences from other fellow Naga tribes in spite of an affinity amongst them.
3. Sometimes it is difficult to maintain unity among the sub-tribes. There are clashes of interests and leadership.
4. Traditional social practices like headhunting have infused enmity and suspicion among the sub-tribes.

It is so deeply rooted that it is still lingering in their minds.

5. Illiteracy is also another factor.
6. The policy of the Indian Government towards the Nagas is characterized by lack of awareness. There is always a gap between the policies and the realities of the situation. Hence any agreement or accord serves the purpose of a temporary subsidence.
7. Some of the Naga leaders were also responsible for omission and commission.
8. Some of the agreements were concluded under duress, hence within no time it falls like a house of cards, e.g. 9 Points Agreement.
9. Some of the accords were concluded by some section of people without the knowledge of the general public. Hence it is bound to perish shortly e.g. Shillong Accord, 1975.

Let us discuss some of the Agreements and Accords in order to understand the Naga problem.

5.1 The Nine Point Agreement: (The Hydari Agreement of 1947)

This agreement was arrived at between the Naga National Council and the Governor of Assam in June 1947.[1]

In the preamble, it says, "The Right of the Nagas to develop themselves according to their freely expressed wishes is recognized".

This was the first agreement concluded between the NNC and the Government of India. It was the time when India faced lots of problems economically and politically, shattered by the Second World War. And this was also a time when the integration of India as a whole was threatened by the secessionist group to secede from the so called Indian mainstream.

Some of the Naga leaders knew that when the British left India there would be political confusion. They also knew that the Naga political problem would remain unsolved. So they submitted a memorandum to the British Government to leave the Nagas as it was before the coming of the British. The visualization of the Naga leaders came true. The Naga problem became a major issue. Sir Akbar Hydari, the then Governor of Assam visited Kohima on June 27, 28, 1947 and had long discussion with the NNC. Thereafter an agreement known as "9 Points Agreement" was concluded under duress. According to Phizo's letter to Shri C. Rajagopala-chari, the then Governor General of India, (a letter from Presidency Jail, Calcutta, 22 November, 1948). "The proposed agreement better known as the"Governor"s ten years agreement" (Hydari Agreement) provided for an interim Government for ten years as demanded by the Nagas. It was fully discussed in February, 1947. At that time, fourth fifth of the members of the NNC were government servants. It was in June 1947, under duress of high Indian officials the NNC was divided Sir Pawsey, the last British D.C. was there. As most of the NNC members were government servants it was accepted. During the discussion of the agreement, Sir Akbar Hydari threatened the Nagas with military power in the presence of Sir Pawsey and others. Within three days the Naga public rejected Sir Akbar Hydari's agreement. His threat was considered as a challenge and it enraged the people".[2]

On the other hand, the Government of India did not implement the agreement. In the agreement, the NNC was given full power to exercise its control over important subjects. The most controversial point was article 9 which was about the period of agreement.'[3] If we correlate this with the preamble of the very agreement i.e. "The right of the Nagas to develop themselves according to their freely expressed wishes is recognized", it is very clear that, at the end of the ten years period, the Nagas have the freedom to decide their own destiny, to be within the Constitution of India or outside it.

The agreement failed to serve any purpose mainly due to its vagueness, and also because of the various interpretations given to the article No. 9.

The failure of the 9 points agreement was the beginning of the wrong tract of the Naga political movement. Since then, it may be said that the dark hour has just set in the paradise like-country of the Nagas.

5.2 The Sixteen Point Agreement

This agreement was arrived at between the Naga people Convention and the Government of India in July 1960.[4] Before we discuss the sixteen point agreement, let us try to know something about the NPC organization.

'The undeclared war between the Nagas and the Indian Government began in 1955. Since then, there has been no peace. Every now and then there came news of fighting, violence and loss of many lives. The Nagas suffered from both sides. The underground Nagas pressed them for supplying financial and other economic necessities. On the other hand, the Indian Government tortured them for helping the underground Nagas. There was discontentment among some section of the Nagas, within a very short period, many lives were lost. The promise of independent Naga state which seemed to be very near was out of sight. The innocent villagers were badly treated by the military forces especially in late 1950s. Violence, killing and atrocities such as arrests, beating and burning of villages became the normal routine. The Naga leaders sent a message to the

Indian Prime Minister saying "You have grossly betrayed us, but we warn you the Naga nation will never surrender". The Indian Government said that "it is the problem of law and order caused by some few Naga people". In the midst of this uncertainty, some Naga leaders convened a meeting known as the Naga Peoples Convention (NPC) in 1957 to act as a mediator between the Government of India and the underground sympathizers. Of these, a few were heartily sick of the bloodshed, between 1955 and 1957. There were others who wished to gain name and fame by striking a deal with the Government of Nagaland".[5]

The intention of the NPC was to create a conducive atmosphere so that the Government of India and the underground Nagas could come together and find out a negotiated settlement through direct talk. But at this juncture, it is very difficult to do that until and unless the mediator is good enough to understand both the parties. Moreover, it should be free from selfish pride motives and uprising emotional mentality. Patience is another necessity. But the NPC lacked some of these elements. Obviously, the NPC miserably failed. "With the widening rift between the underground Nagas and the NPC, we witness the clear emergence of a third group namely NPC itself".[6] The NPC was convinced that it could not please both the parties and solve the problem. But they have to go ahead as it looked forward to do something. They thought that the India Government would not concede the demand of the underground Nagas. So they wanted to 'bargain with the Government of India. Thus, the Naga People Convention appointed a Drafting Committee to formulate a policy for bringing about settlement without the Federal Government of Nagaland. The Drafting Committee prepared a 16 point memorandum. The memorandum was discussed in the third Naga People's Convention in October 1959 at Mokokchung. The Draft was endorsed by it. The NNC regarded this as a "traitor" to the present body NNC. This 16 points draft memorandum was presented to the Governor in Shillong. There were bitter opposition and protest by the Nagas. But the NPC delegates went ahead and the memorandum was submitted to the Prime Minister of India. An agreement based on this memorandum was concluded in July 1960.[7]"

Dr. Imkongliba Ao was the Chairman and Architect of the NPC. He was a medical Doctor by profession. Because of his role in concluding the 16 points agreement which was against the wishes of the underground Nagas, he was assassinated in August 1961.

According to article 2 of the agreement, the Minister in-charge of the Nagas was placed under the Ministry of External affairs of the Government of India. Article 16 states that the Inner line Regulation and Rules embodied in the Bengal Eastern Frontier Regulation 1873 shall remain in force in Nagaland.

But the agreement was not acceptable to the prominent leaders. "In the meanwhile, Phizo, the NNC President who was staying in England sent a message, saying that he did not recognize the New Delhi-NPC pact as having any bearing whatsoever on the Naga political issue and branded the NPC leaders as "Indian Puppet Master".[8]

The conclusion of the 16 points agreement could not solve the problem, nor could it bring peace in the Naga area because of the following reasons:

1. It was not consensus agreement.
2. The NPC was not the right organization to be consulted in solving the Nagas problem. Its role was supposed to be that of a mediator for creating a conducive environment. But later on, it acted as a parent body and worked in its own way.

3. The creation of the State of Nagaland could not solve the problem of the Nagas as a whole.

The following are some of the conclusion of the 16 points agreement:

1. Granting of Statehood (Nagaland State).
2. Emergence of a strong overground element.
3. Division among the extremists and emergence of Pro-New Delhi group.

The agreement failed to solve the Naga problem nor could bring a complete peace to the state of Nagaland.

5.3 Shillong Accord

Shillong accord was again another step taken by some of the Naga leaders to bring peace to the strife-torn state of Nagaland.

The 16 points agreement was concluded in 1960, but there was no complete peace. The situation hardly improved. In this atmosphere, some of the Christian leaders including Rev. Michael Scott, a British citizen initiated a direct talk between the underground Nagas and the Indian Government leaders. An agreement was signed by both the parties on August 15, 1964. It was officially christened as "Cease-fire" and came into force with effect from September 6, 1964. Some of the important provisions of the agreement were:

The Indian security forces will not undertake

(a) Jungle operation
(b) Raiding of underground Camps
(c) Patrolling beyond one thousand yards of security posts.
(d) Searching of villages

(e) Ariel action

(f) Arrest and

(g) Imposition of labor by way of punishment.

The underground Nagas also agreed to observe the following conditions:

(a) Stoppage of sniping and ambushing

(b) Abandonment of kidnapping and recruitment

(c) No sabotage activities

(d) No raiding and firing on security posts, towns and administrative centre and

(e) No moving with arms or in uniform in towns, villages and administrative centre wherever there are security posts, and no approaching within one thousand yards of a security post.

Negotiations for political settlement began from September 23, 1964, at Chedema Peace Camp. This negotiation between the Government of India and the underground was hitherto called "Peace talk". This peace talk had two phases, the first was at the Government level and there were as many as seven rounds of talks at this level; the second was at the Ministerial level spreading over six rounds of talks.[9]

But the high hope of maintaining peace after signing the Cease-fire was not achieved. After a few months, the political picture in Nagaland as well as the cease fire areas of Manipur became uncertain as fresh arms confrontation took place. There were frequent breaches of the spirit of the Cease-fire agreement by both the parties in the form of fighting, raids and imposition of fines on the villages. While fighting was on by the underground Nagas, some of the Christian leaders, under the banner of the NPC (Nagaland

Peace Council) tried their best to bring peace in Nagaland. On August 8, 1974, the NPC submitted a memorandum to L. P. Singh, the then Governor, in a bid to explore a fresh approach for a final political settlement of the Nagas. On August 27, 1974, a public meeting was held at Kohima, Nagaland. The meeting was attended by the Naga Public Peace Conferences by sending five representatives from each tribe, sixteen representatives from various Christian associations and conventions, besides public leaders from both NNO and UDP parties. They endorsed the call earlier given by the Nagaland Peace council and urged the underground Nagas and the Government of India to come to an early political settlement, and thereby avoid further bloodshed. But both the underground Nagas and the Indian Government did not give a positive response to the proposals. Moreover, the Government of India was not ready to negotiate unless the Nagas give up their secessionist demand.

The Nagaland Peace Council in 1974 was quite different from the previous peace mission of 1964. It was less publicized. It was working almost quietly and there was no press report on its activities.

In September 1975, the liaison committee of the Nagaland Peace Council was able to bring the top underground leaders to the well known Chedema Peace Camp under the "Safe conduct arrangement". The Council adumbrated two principles namely, (1) the solution should be "honorable" to all concerned and that (2) it should be "acceptable to both sides. So the council was instrumental in bringing the two sides together in early November 1975 for a talk. The six member underground delegation led by Kevi Yallya (Phizo's brother) met L.P Singh in November 10, 1975 at Raj Bhavan, Shillong. The meeting was held in Camera. There was no press conference and no hair-splitting discussion on political matters, unlike the previous talks. The whole show was more in the nature of business meeting."[10]

The following was the outcome of the discussion and was signed on November 11, 1975. It was known as "Shillong Accord".

The followings are the provisions of the Accord:[11]

1. The representatives of the underground organization decided of their own volition to accept without condition the Constitution of India.
2. It was agreed that the arms, now under the underground would be brought out and deposited at appointed places. Details for giving effect to this agreement would be worked out between them and the representatives of the Government, the security forces and members of the Liaison committee.
3. It was agreed that the representatives of the underground organization should have reasonable time to formulate other issues for discussion for a final settlement.

Many people did not consider the 'Shillong Accord' as an accord between the underground Nagas and Government of India. Their arguments are given below:

1. It was not consensus accord. It was concluded by some sections of the leaders. The leaders of warring parties were not informed or involved.
2. It was an unconditional surrender of a few leaders, rather than an accord.

This is to note that the timing of the conclusion of the accord was not favorable to the Nagas. They were facing lots of problems and out of desperation, they were pressurized from both sides. The following are some of the factors responsible for the conclusion of the accord:

1. Nagas suffered a lot of fightings with the India Government for more than two decades. Hence out of desperation, some leaders tried to bring peace by any means. So they reached an agreement which was almost tantamount to unconditional surrender.
2. Since 1973 the Nagas were divided on political issues.
3. A section of the Nagas led by the NNC party was opposed to the violent movement of the underground Nagas.
4. There were pressures from every angles, especially from the Indian Government for choosing either peaceful settlement or facing the consequences.
5. The Chinese supported the Naga movement, but their support was only to provide small arms, and giving training. Their high hope of getting a help from the Chinese was not materialized.

The followings are the results of the Accord:

1. The captured underground Nagas were released.
2. Emergency which was imposed in Nagaland was lifted.
3. The Indian Government suspended unlawful activities Prevention Act 1967.
4. Emergence of a New Party: Before signing this accord, the NNC was the only authentic political organization of the Nagas. This accord had resulted in the emergence of a new organization of the Nagas under the name National Socialist Council of Nagaland (NSCN).
5. This accord infused the seed of division among the Nagas. The United front behind the Naga political movement became a divided house.

To sum up the Accord: The Shillong Accord was initiated and concluded by some of the Naga leaders seeing the mounting woes faced by the Nagas for more than two decades Thus, to realize permanent peace, they surrendered unconditionally. But the situation was hardly improved. Although it gave a little relief for a while, within no time there was a voice of condemnation from every nook and corner. As the seed of Nationalism had already been sown, nothing could stop its growth.

The Shillong Accord gave a death blow to the Naga political movement in general, and NNC in particular. But somehow the movement could survive. This accord added more problems to the already existing complicated issues.

In short, the Shillong Accord tried to eliminate the Naga political issue by surrendering unconditionally. But this proved to be a failure. Because a more forceful with vision rooted and ideology sprang out in the Naga political scene in 1980 under the banner of National Socialist Council of Nagaland (NSCN).

REFERENCES

1. Refer full text.
2. Nandita, Luingam Luithui, Nagaland file. Lancer International New Delhi 1984, p. 51.
3. Refer full text.
4. Refer full text of the agreement.
5. M. Horam Naga Insurgency, Cosmo Publication New Delhi, 1988, p. 82.
6. Ibid., p. 84.
7. Read full text.
8. M. Horam Naga Insurgency Cosmo Publication, New Delhi. 1988, p. 85.

9. M. Horam. Naga insurgency, Cosmo Publication, New Delhi, 1988, p. 110.

10. Ibid., p. 177.

11. 11. Nandita Haksar and Luingam Luithui, Nagaland file, By Lancer International. New Delhi, 1984, p. 159.

6

Present Trends

The Shillong accord hit hard the NNC in particular and the Nagas political movement in general. But the Naga movement somehow managed to escape and shoot up from a corner. In fact, the NNC tried to solve the Naga problem through the Shillong Accord.

The NSCN (Nationalist Socialist Council of Nagaland) under the leadership of Isak Chisi Swu and Th. Muivah emerged as an active organisation for the cause of Naga Independence. Many agreements and accords were concluded but failed to solve the Naga issue completely. The programme and the ideology of the NSCN may be discussed as follows:

The preface of the Manifesto and polarisation of NSCN, 1980 states, "It is, however, to be admitted that notwithstanding the act of patriotism and valor, Nagas found themselves being self defeated now and then. It is purely due to in the first place, parochialism practice in the highest circle of National affairs. In the next path the people have to tread was not illuminated; the sine quanon of clarity of the way to their salvation was absent".[1]

The group headed by Isak-Muivah formed a new party called the National Socialist Council of Nagaland. The group denounced the leadership of Phizo because of the following. reasons.

1. Phizo's long absence from Nagaland, staying away in a foreign land, was one of the reasons. The NSCN manifesto says "that a particular leader staying in a foreign land has sustained the existence of Nagaland thus far and that he alone will bring the final victory too, needs immediate correction".[2]
2. Phizo refused to condemn the Shillong Accord although people urged him to do so.

They formed an alternative Government, Christened "people's Republic of Nagaland" and came out with a strong worded statement condemning the Shillong Accord 1975 as "Accord at treason of 1975". The manifesto goes on to say "True fact must be admitted and it is a facts that the most ignominious sell- out made in the history on the Naga people ever since the time of the first bullet of freedom fired is beyond dispute, the notorious "Shilong Accord ".That Accord definitely deserved 'an outright official and open condemnation.'[3]

"They reaffirmed the use of arms to attain their objectives" Politics is successful 'reads their manifesto but only when backed by arms. We are save so long as we fight to save ourselves.[4] The NSCN does not believe that their goal will be attained through peaceful means. They were much influenced by Mao-Tse-Tung, saying;" Political power grows out of the barrel of a gun". In the manifesto, it clearly says that, "we rule out the illusion of saving Nagaland through peaceful means It is arms that will save our nation and ensure freedom to the people". They, therefore, rejected any move to solve Naga issue through peaceful means. The Shillong accord is a good example. In the Manifesto, it says that, "The Shillong accord by virtue of which India claimed Victory is a dead paper. From the relentless resistance of the people totally condemning the Shillong accord and its predecessors, it is proved that any agreement which inclined towards Indian Union is always rejected by the underground Nagas. Hence, they denounced the Shillong Accord completely and termed it a treacherous accord.

6.1 New Uprising

The following are the substances of the Manifesto of NSCN:

6.2 Nagaland and the National Socialist Council

"The world is fast changing, but the Naga National Council has failed to keep peace with the changing condition of time. It does not understand the world and Nagaland; it has isolated itself from the people; it has not promised any future from the danger or the forces of domination, exploitation and assimilation. All the old forces are yielded and are drown without a trace and any contrary claim is just a claim to save one's own face and not to save the Nation. All have fallen and Nagaland remains to be saved. Where is the way to save our Nation? Where is the Council that upholds the cause of the sovereign Nagaland and the solution of the people?"[5]

We declare, we are revolutionary patriots, set no traitorous not reactionary bounds on us. To us Sovereign existence of our country, salvation of our people is Socialism with their spiritual in Christ are eternal and unquestionable. It is because life has meaning and that is freedom alone. Only the revolutionary patriots are diametrically opposed to all the anti-national, anti people forces. Because, we refuse Nagaland to be gotten for gold, wine and women; we refuse Nagaland to be evaluate; for own status. Indeed, our Nagaland shall for ever refuse to perish together with any leadership or organization that has failed and betrayed her cause that has no promise of future for her people. Time moves on, and we have to move along, although the Naga National Council does not for we have to redeem Nagaland. Therefore, in this irreconcilable the council declares.[6]

6.3 National Existence

The NSCN stands for the unquestionable Sovereign right of the Naga people over every inch of Nagaland, wherever it may be and admit of no existence whatever.

6.4 Political Institution

The NSCN for the principle of the people's supremacy, that is, the dictatorship of the people through the National Socialist Council of the people and the practice of democracy within the organization.

6.5 Economic System

The NSCN stands for socialism. Because it is the only social and economic system that does away with exploitation and ensure fair equality to all the people.

6.6 Religion

The NSCN stands for faith in God and the salvation of mankind in Jesus the Christ alone that is "NAGALAND FOR CHRIST". However, the individual freedom of religion shall be safeguarded and the imposition of their faith on others is strictly forbidden.

6.7 Means

The NSCN rules out the illusion of saving Nagaland through peaceful means. It is arms and arms again that will save our nation and ensure freedom to the people.

6.8 Self Reliance and the Policy of the United Front

The NSCN stands for the practice of the principle of the self reliance and for the united front with all the forces that can be united with.

With this Manifesto, the NSCN moved forward for their destination. According to a reliable source, it is learnt that Muivah-Isak group has established official contact with people Liberation Army (Manipur) and Assamese Student leaders and seems to have signed a "Protocol of understanding". Muivah sent a written message to the people of North East India under the caption, "NO MORE DELUSION".[7] Some of the contents are "It is high time to do away radically with the delusion in the paper, Indian Constitutional guarantee of "equality", justice protection and so on and prudently guard against repetition of being befuddled with the sweet promises of New Delhi Bosses". The message continues to say "leave not any longer the fate of our people adrift on the surging waves of the massive Indian domination and exploitation. Blame not the angels not the devils. Be resolute in purpose and undeterred in the face of reverses. Hold on to your Gun. You are not alone; we are your comrades-in-arms. You can count on us".[8]

With this sacrificial and confidence message the NSCN gave new promises to the Naga political movements and emerged as a stronger force having a deeper root.

Prof. M. Horam in his book *Naga Insurgency* comments: "The Indian official and the men in New Delhi seem to be content with a fond hope that the Nagas will not be able to fight any more like before as the younger Nagas have now become accustomed to comfortable life with easy money available to spend on drinks and other pleasures of life. Some Indian officers even go on to remark with clicking their tongues triumphantly like; "Nagas are divided" they have been bought by us with money and wine "Nagas" with a grin on his face he would say "have weakness for wine" and that never will they have the courage and willingness to go to the inhospitable jungles and fight an army".[9] But this comment of the Indian officers was proved to be wrong.

The Shillong Accord, 1975 was unconditional surrender within the Constitution of India. This Accord seems to be the end of the Naga political movement, but the movement has revived again. It is something like burying a seed in the soil which seems to have disappeared but within no time, the seed germinates inside the soil and a new plant shoots up. People, all over India are curious as to whether this plant will grow and bear fruit or not. This depends on the environment and circumstances to which it is going to be exposed.

REFERENCES

1. Manifesto and polarization of NSCN. 1980. Preface
2. Ibid., p. 4.
3. Ibid., p. 4.
4. M. Horam. Naga Insurgency, Cosmo Publication New Delhi, 1988 p. 244.
5. Manifesto and Polarisation of NSCN 1980, p. 51.
6. Ibid., p. 53.
7. No more delusion issued by Th. Muivah General Secretary NSCN Dated Oking 2nd July 1980.
8. Ibid.
9. M. Horam Naga Insurgency, Cosmo Publication, New Delhi 1988, p. 245.

7

Conclusion

The Naga political movement is the oldest of all the existing political movements in India. After more than six decades of its existence, there is still no sign of peace or solution. Going through the preceding chapters, and after examining the journey of the Naga political movement, it is seen that the Naga political problem is not decreasing but is increasing adding more problems. This surprises us, but when we examine minutely, we can concede that it is so, because; before the advent of the British, the Nagas did not have the feeling of the sense of modern Nationhood. However each and every village was more or less independent like that of the Greek-City state. But in spite of this, they had the feeling of oneness because of the same affinities and heritage. In the later period through the contact with western countries they became conscious of individual right, social right, and national right, and also the right to self determination which are incorporated in the UN Charter. Hence, steadily, they have gathered greater momentum for realizing and demanding their rights.

Secondly, the Naga political problem is increasing because any step taken up by the Indian Government to solve the Naga political problem was not carried out honorably by both sides. Hence it adds more problems to the burning issue.

Thirdly, the contemporary young Naga research Scholars found no relation of the Naga with the Indians or the Naga areas being a part of India historically. Hence the restless youth want to revive the past history. This attitude grew stronger within the Naga community.

Fourthly, the Nagas think that the British policy excluding the Naga from the rest of the Indian administration is the sign of Nagas being different from the Indian. This also strengthened their sentiment.

Fifthly, there is youth unrest due to rampant corruption, unemployment, nepotism and favoritism etc. in civil administration and the reign of military terror, violation of Human rights, torture and assault on women and other inhuman treatment added more fuel to the burning problem. Hence the seed of hatred is sown and the feeling of separatism has been intensified among the Nagas.

Because of all these reasons, the Naga political movement could not come to an end but is culminating to a bigger flame. Apart from this, the credit of the genesis of the Naga Political movement goes to the advent of Christianity. In fact Christianity was the root cause of awakening and development of the Nagas areas. It provides education and leadership, imbibing and infusing new blood into every Nagas. It is education through the advent of Christianity which produced leadership. This factor is responsible for unifying the Nagas by inculcating political consciousness among the Nagas and making them work for a good common goal. It is opined that the Naga political issue is a multidimensional issue, touching the social, economic and political aspects. But there are some people who say that it is only a political issue, whereas the rest are minor elements under which grievances culminated into a movement. Hence, it is a political issue only. But before we give our opinion and conclude what really is, it will be good to know the demand of the Underground Nagas. The Nagas says that they do not ask for "Secession" but demand for "recognition" of their *separate* entity which was there from the time immemorial. It further said that she was annexed to Indian Union under duress. If we judge from this angle, the Naga problem can be termed only as a political issue. But controversy is still there which is not free from criticism.

The Nagas are firmly convinced that their way of life has something to offer which other people or system could not give her. Such kind of feeling makes them proud of their cultural heritage.

We may summarize some of the short comings of both sides i.e. the Indian Government and the Nagas movement.

1. The mistrust and unfaithfulness characterized attitudes of both the parties, Indian Government and the leaders of the underground Nagas fail to materialize the issue. This was mainly responsible for the failure of the "Peace talks" in the 60's.
2. The Nagas on their side had too many leaders. Some of them were part-time politicians, others, city crier, and some others were mere opportunists. The Indian Government took the advantage of such opportunity.
3. The internal disorder, disunity of the underground Nagas group is another setback. Such rivalry led to the murder of T. Sakhrie, the General Secretary of the NNC. Such an act gives a great stumbling block to the Naga's political movement.
4. The long absence of Phizo, the leader of the Nagas, from the Naga soil weakened the movement.
5. The Government of India felt that the Naga movement could be suppressed by force. However this was proved wrong. The Nagas could be won by

love and not by force. This had been proved by the past history.

6. Both the Indian Government and some of the Naga leaders failed to know that an accord or an agreement which is not honored by both sides or which is not concluded by consensus will bring more harm than good.
7. The Naga movement is not actively participated by the whole community of the Nagas. Some people in the remote areas, especially in the villages, hardly know the movement so are not serious about it. This was due to lack of political consciousness and facility of mass media etc.
8. The Indian Government on the other hand, displays glaring and paramount lack of awareness, understanding about the Nagas and its unique history and callousness in dealing with the Naga problem. They see the Naga issue as mere law and order problem.

   The Government of India is always suspicious of the Nagas and thereby reacts in a naive manner.
9. The short-sighted policy of the Indian Government affects the Nagas. This indirectly brings into existence economic disparity in the society. It is said that, "Financing does not buy gratitude, and gratitude does not assure friendship".
10. The high-handedness of the Indian security forces does not improve the situation, but rather it worsens it.

Because of all these reasons the Naga political movement remains unsolved without finding settlement. Moreover, it seems that the gap between the underground Nagas and the Indian Union is becoming wider and wider leading to an 'unbridgeable one'.

7.1 IMPACT

Any historical process has an impact on the social and political life and progress of the people. And the movement like the Nagas has a tremendous impact in social, economic and political life of its people. This movement had both positive and negative impact. To mention some in brief, on the positive side, the Naga movement dawns a new political consciousness among the Nagas. This consciousness made the Nagas more cohesive and integrated. This feeling of oneness keeps away inter-Naga and inter-village feuds. This movement also results in creation of Nagaland State and received a lot of attention from the Central Government. The creation of Nagaland State is a blessing in one way. In the economic field, there is no denying the fact that input for development scheme are provided for the upliftment of the Nagas. The living condition of the people has improved through these development schemes.

This is one side of the coin, but the other side of the same coin is different. The Naga political movement has a negative impact too. Some of them are given below.

Many innocent people were victimized. The brutal act of the military forces towards the Nagas sowed the seed of hatred and suspicion. Thus, the Nagas and the rest of Indians are segregated from one another. Secondly, the huge amount of financial grants given to the State of Nagaland has created a distinct economic disparity. Earlier there were no economic classes in Naga society. But with the creation of Nagaland State and pouring of huge amount of money from the Central Government, there has emerged economic social classes dividing the society into two classes i.e. rich and poor. Along with this comes corruption. Thirdly, party politics has been characterized by factionalism. These further divide the Nagas and weaken the society.

To conclude, I would like to say that, in spite of the many gestures made by the Government so far, there is yet to solve the Naga issue permanently. Things are dragging on in an atmosphere of virtual stalemate. And in spite of much initiative from both sides, peace, ceasefire etc., becomes an empty slogan. It seems that different accords and agreements have deceived one and all. How long will this continue? Only time will tell.

We have learnt from past history that the Naga problem cannot be solved through military force. We must not forget that Nagaland is a border state with Burma. The border is impossible to seal at any expenditure of time and energy. And we must also not forget that Nagaland occupies a strategic importance for India from the security point of view as many foreign countries are lying close by. It is for this reason that the Naga problem should be solved rationally at the earliest, and the settlement should be honorable to both sides.

Appendices

Naga Memorandum to Simon Commission

To, Dated, 10th January, 1929.

The British Statutory Commission

Camp India

Subject: Memorandum of the Naga Hills

Sir,

We the undersigned Nagas Club at Kohima, who are the only persons at present who can voice for our people have heard with great regret that our Naga Hills is included within the Reformed Scheme of India without our knowledge, but as administration of our Hill is continued to be in the hands of British Officers and we did not consider it necessary to raise any protest in the past. Now we learnt that you have come to India as representative of the British Government to enquire into the working of the system of Government and the growth of education and we beg to submit below our view with the prayer that our Hills may be withdrawn from the Reformed Scheme and placed outside the Reforms but directly under British Government. We never asked for any reforms and we do not wish for any reforms.

Before the British Government conquered our Country in 1879-80, we were living in a state of intermittent warfare with the Assamese of the Assam Valley to the North and West of our Country and Manipuri's to the South. They never conquered us, nor were we ever subjected to their rule. On the other hand, we were always a terror to these people. Our Country within the administered area consists of more than eight regions quite different from one another, with quite different languages which cannot be understood by each other, and there are more regions outside the administered area which are not known at present. We have no unity among us and it is only the British Government that is holding us together now.

Our education is poor. The occupation of our Country by the British Government being so recent as 1880, we have had no chance or opportunity to improve in education and though we can boast of two or three graduates of an Indian University in our Country, we have not got one yet who is able to represent all our different regions small in comparison with the population of the plains districts in the Province; and any representation that may be allotted to us in the council will be negligible and will have no weight whatever. Our language is quite different from those of the plains and we have no social affinities with the Hindus or Musalmans. We are looked down upon by the one for "beef" and the other for our "pork" and by both for our want in education, is not due to any fault of our.

Our Country in poor and it does not pay for its administration. Therefore, if it is continued to be placed under the Reformed Scheme, we are afraid that new and heavy taxes will have to be imposed on us, and when we cannot pay, then all lands will have to be sold and in the long run we shall have no share in the land of our birth and life will not be worth living then. Though our land at present is within the British territory, government have always recognized our private rights in it, but is we are forced to enter the council the majority of whose number is sure to belong to the other customs to supersede our own customary laws which we now enjoy.

For the above reasons, we pray that the British Government will continue to safeguard our right against all encroachment from other people who are more advanced than us by withdrawing our country that we should not be thrust to the mercy of other people who could never be subjected; but to leave us alone to determine ourselves as in ancient times. We claim not only the members of the "Naga Club" to represent all those regions to which we belong viz. Angamis, Kacha Nagas, Kukis, Semas, Lothas, and Rengma but also other regions of Nagaland.

Signed by:

1. Nihu, Angami, Head Interpreter;
2. Hisale, Peshkar;
3. Nishar Angami, Master;
4. Khosa, Doctor;
5. Gebo Kacha Naga, Interpreter;
6. Vipunyu Angami, Potdar;
7. Goyiepra Angami, Treasurer;
8. Ruzhukhrie Angami, Master;
9. Dikrie Angami, Sub-Overseer;
10. Zapuzhulie Angami, Master;
11. Zepulie Angami, Interpreter;
12. Katsuno Angami, Interpreter;
13. Nuolhoukielie Angami, Interpreter;
14. Inzevi Sema, Interpreter;
15. Apano Lotha, Interpreter;

16. Resile Rengma, Interpreter;
17. Lengjang Kuki, Interpreter;
18. Nikhriehu Angami, Interpreter;
19. Miakrao Angami, Chaprasi;
20. Levi Kacha Naga, Clerk.

The Yehzabo of Nagaland Preamble

We, the people of Nagaland, solemnly acknowledging that the sovereignty over tills earth and the entire universe belongs to Almighty God alone, and the authority of the people to be exercised on the territory is a sacred trust from our people through the years of trial, and

Having our attachment to the truth of popular sovereignty as declared on 22nd March 1956, and in the articles in the provisional Yehzabo of 1962, and following the amended Yehzabo of 1968, to establish national institutions based on the common ideals of democracy, justice, liberty, equality and fraternity among the people composing it,

Do hereby adopt in our National Assembly the (Amended) Yehzabo of Nagaland this 6th March in the year of our Lord Nineteen Hundred and Seventy One.

PART I

1. The territory of Nagai and shall comprise all the territories inhabited by the indigenous Naga Tribes and such other territories as Tatar Hoho may, by law, admit on such terms and conditions as it deems fit.
2. This Yehzabo shall apply to the territories as defined in Article I.

3. (a) Nothing in the Yehzabo or by any law shall allow any tribe to secede from the Nation.

   (b) The Tatar Hoho shall, from time to time, make laws for ensuring and preserving the unity and integrity of the Nation.

4. Each village is a republic having its territory, full authority over its own affairs including land, community organization, social and religion, customs and practices.

5. Each area or territory inhabited by the communities of a tribe shall be constituted into a federated Unit to be called a Region and each of the Regions shall be given autonomy to the extent of management of local affairs and administration.

6. Some persons or group of persons belonging to others communities living in such area or territory which is inhabited predominantly by a larger tribe or community, shall be duly associated along with the day of the British shall continue to have legal recognition of this Yehzabo.

7. The name of the National Government shall continue to be calling "THE FEDERAL GOVERNMENT OF NAGALAND".

PART II
CITIZENSHIP AND RIGHTS OF CITIZENS

8. There shall be but one citizenship throughout Nagaland, that is to say, there shall be no citizenship of the Unit as distinct from that of the Nation.

9. At the commencement of this Yehzabo any person who was a citizen of Nagaland immediately before the commencement of the amended Yehzabo shall become and be a citizen of Nagaland.

10. Notwithstanding the provision contained in Article 10, nothing in the Yehzabo shall derogate the power of the Tatar Hoho to make such laws for admission of new classes of citizens or for the termination of the citizenship of any existing classes.

11. All citizens irrespective of birth, religion, sex or race shall be equal before the eyes of the law.

12. There shall be no discrimination against any citizen in political, economic and social relations because of social status of family origin.

13. There shall be equality of opportunity for all citizens in matters of public employment, appointment, promotion and recruitment, irrespective of clan, tribe and family origin.

14. No titles other than academic distinction shall be recognized by any citizen of Nagaland except with the approval of the Government.

15. Free profession and practice of religion shall be guaranteed to any citizen.

16. Subject to the security of Nagaland, public order, morality, contempt of Court and defamation, all citizens shall have the right to enjoy freedom of speech and expression, to form assembly and association, to move freely throughout Nagaland, to carry on any procession and to use, enjoy and dispose of any property in accordance with local usage and practice.

PART ILL
EXECUTIVE

17. There shall be a President of Nagaland.

18. The Executive power of the Federal Government of Nagaland shall be vested in the President and shall

be exercised by him with the Council of Kilonsers in accordance with the provisions of this Yehzabo and laws.

19. The President shall be elected by an electoral college consisting of the elected members of the Tatar Hoho.

20. The President shall hold Office for a term of 3 (three) years from the date on which he enter upon his office.

21. The President shall be removed from Office on impeachment for violation of the Yehzabo and conviction of treason, sedition, bribery or other high crimes and misdemeanours.

22. (a) The President shall, by writing under his own hand addressed to the Vice-President, resign his Office. Any resignation addressed to the Vice-President shall forthwith be communicated by him to the Speaker of the Tatar Hoho.

    (b) If the Office of the President is caused vacant the election to fill the vacant seat shall be completed before the expiration of that term.

23. The President shall, after the expiration of his term, continue to hold Office until his successor enters upon his Office.

24. Any citizen of Nagaland who is born of Naga blood and has completed 40 (forty) years of age, and is qualified for election as a member of Tatar Hoho, shall be eligible for election to the Office of the President.

25. Any person who holds or has held Office of the President shall be eligible for re-election for the Office for more terms.

26. Every person acting as President or discharging the function of the President shall, before entering upon his Office, make and subscribe the following oath in the

presence of the Chief Justice of Supreme Court or any person appointed in that behalf: "I .... do solemnly declare and affirm that I will faithfully execute the Office of the President of Nagaland, and will, to the best of my ability, preserve, protect and defend the Yehzabo of Nagaland and that I will dedicate wholly myself to serve the service and welfare of the people of Nagaland.

27. When a President is to be impeached as defined in Art 22, a proposal shall be moved in the form of resolution in writing signed by not less than one-fourth of the tata-1 number of the house. When such a resolution has been passed by a majority of not less than 2/3 (two-third) membership of the House, Such resolution shall have the effect of removing the President from his Office, with effect from the date on which the resolution is so passed.

28. In case of the removal of the President from Office, or of his death or resignation, the Vice-President shall act as Acting President, until a fresh Presidential election takes place.

29. (a) The President shall be the Supreme Commander, of Armed Forces of Nagaland, and

    (b) In exercise of his powers as Supreme Commander, the President shall have power to issue directives for disposition of Armed Forces, for planning and execution of military campaigns, to deal with emergencies like foreign invasion and any matter appertaining to the conduct of war.

    (c) The President shall have the power to confer commissions on the Office of Armed Forces.

    (d) The President shall not have the power either to declare war or conclude peace without the consent of the Tatar Hoho.

30. The President shall have the power to grant pardon and reprieve, to suspend or remit or commute the sentence of any person convicted in criminal offences.

31. (a) The President shall have the right to exercise Emergency Powers when the security of Nagaland or any part thereof is threatened by external aggression, internal disturbances or failure of constitutional machinery.

    (b) In exercise of the foregoing powers the President shall issue Ordinances by proclamations and use such forces for meeting the situation for a period of six months unless extended by Tatar Hoho.

32. The President shall also have power to exercise such extraordinary powers which the Tatar Hoho may, from time to time, empower him to exercise.

VICE PRESIDENT

33. There shall be a Vice President of Nagaland.

34. The Vice President shall be elected in accordance with the provision contained in Article 20.

35. The Vice President shall hold Office for a term on (three) years from the date on which he enter upon his Office.

36. The Vice President shall be removed from his Office on impeachment in accordance with the provisions contained in Articles 22 and 28.

37. (a) The Vice President shall, by writing under his own hand addressed to the President, resign his Office.

    (b) If the Office of the Vice President is caused vacant, election to fill the vacant seat shall be completed before the expiration of that term.

38. The qualification for election to the Office of Vice President shall be the same as the provision contained in Article 25.

39. If and when a member of the Tatar Hoho is elected to the Office of the Vice President he shall after his election be deemed to have vacated his seat in the house.

40. The Vice President shall, before entering upon his Office, make and subscribe, before the President or a person appointed in that behalf, the following oath - "I.......... do solemnly declare and affirm that I will faithfully execute the Office of the Vice President of Nagaland, and I will faithfully discharge the functions and duties conferred on me by the Yehzabo and the laws".

41. The Vice President shall, during the absence of the President from his Office, discharge and perform the powers and functions of the President as Acting President.

PART IV
COUNCIL OF KILONSERS

42. There shall be a Council of Kilonsers, with equal status, to aid and advise the President in exercise of his powers and functions.

43. (a) The Council of Kilonsers shall consist of such numbers as may be determined by Tatar Hoho from time to time from amongst its members and shall hold office for a term on (three) years.

    (b) There shall be Deputy Kilonsers to assist the Council of Kilonsers.

44. The Council of Kilonsers shall perform and discharge such duties and functions as may be assigned to them by the President collectively or individually from time to time.

45. The President shall preside in the meeting of the Council of Kilonsers and shall have the right to vote in case of a tie.

46. A Kilonsers or Deputy Kilonsers shall remain in Office till the expiration of his term, unless:

    (a) He is removed from the Office by a resolution of the House on ground of his inefficiency or committing such offences against the Yehzabo or the state.

    (b) He resigns on ground of personal disability.

47. Any member of Tatar Hoho when he is elected to the Office of Kilonsers or Deputy Kilonsers shall be deemed not to have vacated his seat in the House.

48. Every Kilonsers or Deputy Kilonsers before entering upon his Office, shall make before the President or a person appointed in that behalf the following oath - "I.......... do solemnly declare and affirm that I will faithfully and sincerely perform the duties assigned to me to the best satisfaction of the people of Nagaland".

49. There shall be a Central Secretariat headed by a Secretary General. Establishment of the Central secretariat shall be regulated by law.

TATAR HOHO (PARLIAMENT)

50. There shall be a Federal Parliament consisting of one House known as Tatar Hoho (National Parliament).

51. All the legislative powers of Nagaland shall be vested in the Tatar Hoho.

52. The Tatar Hoho shall be composed of:

(a) Representatives of the Regions elected by the people thereof, on proportionate population, on the basis of one representative per 15,000 populations. Notwithstanding clause (a) any region or regions whose population is less than 15, 000, shall send one representative to the Tatar Hoho.

(b) Two members to be nominated by the President.

53. (a) Any Naga citizen who has completed 25 (twenty five) years of age and is not otherwise disqualified by the law of the land shall be eligible for election to the Tatar Hoho.

54. Every Tatar elected to the Tatar Hoho shall, before taking his seat, take the oath before the Speaker in the following prescribed manner: "I, ... solemnly and truly declare and affirm that I will be faithful and bear allegiance to the Federal Government of Nagaland dedicating wholly myself to the service of the Nation".

55. (a) The Tatar Hoho shall be summoned to meet at least twice in every year.

(b) Nothing in the Yehzabo shall preclude the President to call emergency session of Tatar Hoho.

56. (a) The Hoho shall, unless sooner dissolved, continue for two years and at the expiration of the said period it shall be deemed to have been dissolved.

(b) Notwithstanding clause (a) of this Article, during operation of Emergency by proclamation, the said period may be extended by Tatar Hoho for a period of six months. Provided further, if the operation of Emergency is ended, the extended period shall also be reduced.

57. The Tatar Hoho shall, from amongst its members, choose one Speaker and one Deputy Speaker.

58. (a) The Deputy Speaker, in the absence of the Speaker shall preside over the session and shall conduct the business of the House.

    (b) In case of the dissolution of the Hoho, the Speaker and Deputy Speaker shall continue to hold their respective Office until the newly elected Hoho assembles

59. (a) There shall be a secretariat department.

    (b) The Secretariat or Secretary shall be appointed by the President on the advice of the speaker. Non- Tatars are qualified for the appointment.

    (c) The Secretaries or Secretary shall be responsible for the business of the House.

60. The Tatar Hoho shall make the rule of procedure and the conduct of business in the House.

61. 2/3 (two-thirds) in case of general session and 1/4 (one-fourth) in case of Emergency of the total number of members in the Tatar Hoho shall constitute a quorum to transact the business of the House.

62. All matters in the Tatar Hoho shall be decided by a majority of the member present, the Speaker or any person presiding in the House shall have a casting vote in case of a tie.

63. When a resolution for the removal of the Speaker or the Deputy Speaker from Office is discussed and debated in the House, the Speaker or the Deputy Speaker shall not preside in the House.

64. No person shall be a member of the Tatar Hoho unless he/she is so elected by the Regional Leacy in that behalf.

65. The Tatar Hoho shall have the power to expel any member or members from the house if he/she commits any offence against the House or the State.

66. If a member of the Tatar Hoho is absent from the session for three consecutive sessions without sufficient cause, his/her seat shall be declared vacant.

67. When any seat in the House falls vacant the Speaker shall inform the Regional Leacy concerned with a request to send a new representative to fill the vacancy within a stipulated period.

68. The Regional Leacy shall have the power to withdraw any of its representatives from the Tatar Hoho for want of confidence and shall have power to send a new member in place of the member so withdrawn.

69. (a) No member of the Tatar Hoho shall be prosecuted, arrested, detained or tried for the opinion expressed or vote cast by him in exercise of his function in the House.

    (b) The members of Tatar Hoho shall, except for treason, sedition, felony or breach of peace, be privileged from arrest during the session of the Tatar Hoho.

70. (a) The Tatar Hoho shall have the sole power to try all impeachments. During trials the members who bring the charges of impeachment shall be examined on oath.

    (b) During impeachment no person shall, without the concurrence of 2/3 of the members present, be convicted.

    (c) When the President of Nagaland is impeached the Chief Justice shall preside.

71. Judgment in case of impeachment shall not extend further than removal from Office and disqualification to hold and enjoy any Office of honour or trust under the authority of Nagaland.

LEGISLATIVE PROCEDURE

72. President shall have the right to address the House at the opening session of the Tatar Hoho.

73. The President shall place report and statement (including financial statements) on matters of National or public importance before the House.

74. (a) Every Bill which has been passed by Tatar Hoho shall, before it become a law, be presented to the President for his assent. The President may give his assent to it or send it back with his objection to the House for reconsideration within three months.

    (b) If any Bill is not returned within the stipulated time the same shall be demand to have become law.

75. (a) Any Bill except money deemed to have been introduced by any members in the Tatar Hoho.

    (b) Any Bill shall be deemed to have been passed if it is passed by the House, with or without amendment.

76. (a) A money Bill shall be introduced in Tatar Hoho.

    (b) The President shall prepare estimate of receipts and expenditure of the Government for every financial year and shall present them to the Tatar Hoho for consideration.

77. The submission of estimate of expenditure, the appropriation of the revenues and all other matters

connected there with shall, in so far as provision in not made in that behalf by this Yehzabo be regulated by law made Tatar Hoho as it deems fit.

78. (a) All estimates of expenditure shall be submitted in the form of demands for grants to the Tatar Hoho and the House shall have power to assent to or reject any demand with such requisition of the amount.

(b) No demand for a grant shall be made in the same session except on the recommendation of the President.

79. Notwithstanding anything contained in the foregoing provision the Tatar Hoho shall have power:

(a) To make any grant in advance in respect of the estimated expenditure for a part of any financial year;

(b) To make a grant for meeting an unexpected demands such as for defense or for a military undertaking etc.

80. (a) The Tatar Hoho shall have the power to levy and collect taxes and revenues.

(b) The Tatar Hoho shall also have the power to take loans on the credit of the Government and to pay debt.

81. The Tatar Hoho shall powers to raise and support armies, to provide and maintain service, to lay down rules covering the organization and maintenance of the Military Forces.

82. The Tatar Hoho shall have the power to make laws on the following subjects: Foreign Affairs including entering into treaties, agreement and contracts with other countries, war and peace, communications,

census, all Federal services, audit of accounts of Federal Government, Supreme Court, Elections, Preventive detention, amnesty etc.

PART V
FEDERAL JUDICIARY

83. There shall be a Federal Supreme Court of Nagaland consisting of a Chief Justice and four other judges.

84. The President shall have power, with the advice and consent of the Tatar Hoho, to appoint the Chief Justice and other Judges.

85. Any person who is a citizen of Nagaland and has' special experience and knowledge in legal realm of customs, traditions, social practices or academic laws, shall be eligible to be appointed as Judge of the Supreme Court.

86. A Judge of the Supreme Court or other subordinate Court shall not be removed from Office except for proved misconduct or incapacity.

87. (a) A proposal to prefer a charge for removal of a Judge of the. Supreme Court shall not be adopted by Tatar Hoho except upon a resolution of the House supported by two-thirds majority of members present.

(b) Where a charge is preferred against a Judge, a Special Tribunal, consisting of the members of the Tatar Hoho, shall be appointed to investigate the charge

(c) The decision shall, on the report of the Special Tribunal, be taken by the Tatar Hoho for or against removal of the Judge.

88. The Judges of the Supreme Court shall, while entering upon the Office, take an oath in the manner prescribed

as follows: "I,.......... having been appointed Chief Justice (Judge) of the Supreme Court, do hereby solemnly declare and affirm that I will faithfully and honestly perform the duties assigned to me, and to the best of my knowledge and judgment I shall administer justice to the people of our land and that I will uphold the Yehzabo and the laws".

89. The Supreme Court shall have original jurisdiction over the following matters:

(a) All matters arising under the constitution and involving its interpretations,

(b) Between regions or between the state and the region or regions,

(c) Such other matters, if any as may be defined by law.

90. The Supreme Court shall have appellate jurisdiction from the decision and judgment of the Regional courts, and shall also have appellate jurisdiction from the decision of other tribunals appointed by the Tatar Hoho for exceptional cases.

91. (a) An appeal shall lay to the Supreme court from any judgment, final order or sentence, any criminal proceeding of a Regional Court if the Regional Court certifies that the case is fit for appeal to the Supreme Court.

(b) (i) An appeal shall lay to the Supreme Court from any judgment, decree or final order in a civil proceeding of a Regional Court if the Regional Court certifies that the value of the subject matter of the dispute is not less than Rs 3,000/

(ii) The claim of title respecting property is valued at not less than Rs. 3,000/-.

(iii) Notwithstanding clause (a) and (b) of this Article the Supreme Court shall, in its discretion, grant special leave to appeal from any judgment, sentence or order made by any Regional Court or Tribunal, where, (a) gross injustice has been done in criminal proceedings, (b) in civil cases the question of general interest or public importance is involved.

92. The Supreme Court shall be barred from interfering in any proceeding of cases pending in other courts.

93. The decision, order or judgment made by the Supreme Court shall be binding on all Courts, within the territory of Nagaland.

94. Subject to the provisions of any law made by the Tatar Hoho the Supreme Court shall, with the approval of the Tatar Hoho, be empowered to make rules and procedure of the Court.

PART VI
REGIONAL LEACY

95. There shall be a Regional Leacy for each Region consisting of members elected by Sub-Regional Committee.

96. Each Regional Leacy shall have the right to determine the number of its members.

97. (a) There shall be a Speaker and Secretary in the Leacy elected from amongst its members.

(b) The tenure of Office of the Members in Leacy shall be 3 (three) years with effect from the date on which they enter upon their Office.

98. Any member of the Regional Leacy shall be removed from his Office by two-thirds majority of the members present for offences against the State or the law.

99. The Leacy shall have the power to make legislation on the following matters of local affairs such as:

(a) Maintenance of public order, regional administration, regional finance.

(b) Organization of Sub-regional Committee and Courts.

(c) Reformatory institutions

(d) Public health

(e) Rehabilitation

(f) Land and land development

(g) Agriculture

(h) Water and irrigation

(i) Protection of wild animals

(j) Forest

(k) Gambling.

100. The Regional Leacy shall have the power to make legislation on the matters of local interest which are not specifically enumerated in Article 100, but in case of any inconsistency of the Regional legislation with the Federal Law the latter will prevail.

REGIONAL EXECUTIVE

101. There shall be an Executive Head in a Region called Midan Peyu.

102. The Midan Peyu shall be the Agent of the President and be appointed by the President on the recommendation of the Regional Leacy for a term of three years, and he shall remain in Office till his successor takes over the Office.

103. Any citizen of Nag ala rid shall be eligible to the Office of Midan Peyu.

104. The Executive power and function of the region shall be vested in the Midan Peyu and shall be exercised by him through the Regional Executive.

105. The Midan Peyu shall, in a Region, be responsible to perform the duties towards the Federal Government of Nagaland.

106. There shall be a Regional Executive the number of which shall be determined by the Regional Leacy concerned.

107. The members of the Regional Executive shall be elected by the Regional Leacy from amongst its members.

108. The Regional Executive shall advise and assist the Midan Peyu in discharge of his functions and duties.

SUB-REGIONAL COMMITTEE

109. There shall be more than one Sub-Regional Units in a Region and a Sub-Regional Committee shall be composed of the representatives of Village Councils.

110. The Village Council shall, in the Sub-Regional Committee, be represented by its Runa Peyu or any person authorized in this behalf

111. (a) The Sub-Regional Committee shall have the local administrative powers in the area under the direction of the Regional Leacy, and the

administrative power for the Sub-Regional Unit shall be exercised by the Runa Peyu as its Administrative Head.

(b) The Runa Peyu shall be appointed by the Midan Peyu on the recommendation of the Sub-Regional Committee.

112. The Sub-Regional Committee shall remain subordinate to the Regional Leacy and its functions and duties shall be regulated by the rules made by the Regional Leacy.

113. Notwithstanding the provisions contained in the foregoing Articles 110 and 11, where the formation of Sub-Regional Committee is not practicable the regional Leacy shall have the powers to formulate its own administrative arrangement according to the convenience of the Region concerned.

REGIONAL COURT

114. There shall be a Regional Court for each Region.

115. (a) The number of Judges in the regional Court shall be determined by the Regional Leacy and the Judges shall be appointed by the President on the recommendation and ad vice of the Regional Leacy through Midan Peyu.

(b) The President shall appoint one from amongst the Judges as presiding Chairman of the Court.

116. The Judges shall hold office during their good behaviour in Office.

117. A Judge of the Regional Court shall be removed from the Office for his proved misconduct by a resolution passed by two-thirds majority of the members in the Leacy.

118. The Regional Leacy shall have no power or jurisdiction in the interpretation of the Yehzabo.

119. The Regional Court shall have original jurisdiction on any matter that arises between two or more sub-Regions.

120. The Regional Court shall have appellate jurisdiction to hear disputes on appeals from the decisions, orders or judgment of the Sub-Regional Courts.

121. The Regional Court shall have the power of Superintendence over the Sub-Regional Courts.

SUB-REGIONAL COURT

122. There shall be a Sub-Regional Court for each Sub-Region and the number of Judges shall be determined by the Regional Leacy.

123. The Judges of the Sub-Regional Court shall be elected by the members of the Regional Leacy and the Runa Peyu and shall act as President Officer of the Court.

124. The Sub-Regional Court shall have original jurisdiction over disputes that arise between two or more villages or between persons or groups of persons of different Villages.

125. The Sub-Regional Court shall have appellate jurisdiction over the dispute that arises from the decision of the Village Court.

126. The Village Court shall be the lowest Judicial Court in Nagaland and the administration of Justice shall be regulating according to their customs, traditions and usage.

127. (a) In exercise of the foregoing Article 127, no outside interference shall be allowed by the Yehzabo and by law.

(b) No appeal from the jurisdiction of the Village Court shall be entertained in the Higher Court except a certificate for appeal was granted by the Village Court.

PART VII
OFFICIAL LANGUAGE

128. The Official, Language throughout Nagaland shall be English and all Official business of the Government shall be transacted in English. (Other languages shall be used as medium of common understanding).

129. Regional language shall be used as Official Language in the Region for Official transaction of business of local Government.

PART VIII
DEFENCE

130. The Federal Government of Nagaland shall maintain a standing National Army.

131. The Organization for Defense shall be regulated by the Tatar Hoho in consideration of the situation prevalent in the country.

132. Subject to the provisions of Article 54 (b) the Speaker of Tatar Hoho is empowered to allow Naga Army representatives to participate in the deliberations of the House, particularly on matters of defense.

PART IX
INTERNATIONAL RELATIONS

133. The Federal Government of Nagaland shall maintain Diplomatic Relations with Nations.

134. The relationship of the Federal Government of Nagaland towards all Nations shall be one of peaceful coexistence.

PART X
RELIGION

135. Protestant Christianity and Naga Religion are recognized Religions in Nagaland.

PART XI
YEHZABO

136. The Yehzabo of Nagai and is flexible in nature and as such amendment in respect of any article of Clause can be effected if and when a Bill is passed to that effect by two-thirds majority of Tatar Hoho.

PART XII
POLITICAL ORGANISATION

137. The Naga National Council shall be the only recognized political institution in Nagaland.

138. The Naga National Council shall work on the following principles:

There shall be:

(a) A Central Executive Council which will guide and control the politics and decisions of the Nation.

(b) Regional and Range Council which deal with organizational activities and problems in the respective regions.

Declaration of Naga Independence

Naga National Council declared Naga Independence on 14th August, 1947. Cable to United Nations Secretary General

Cable Runs:

To,

Secretary General

United Nations.

Benign Excellency,

- Kindly put on record that nagas will be independent
- Discussion with India are being carried on to that effect
- Nagas do not accept Indian consititution
- The right of the people must previal regarless of size
- Naga National Council

Note: (This message was acknowledged by UN and record is both in UN and NNC's files).

The Nine Point Agreement, June, 1947

Preamble: The right of the Nagas to develop themselves according to their freely expressed wishes is recognized.

1. Judicial: All cases whether civil or criminal arising between Nagas in the Naga Hills will be disposed of by duly constituted Naga courts according to Naga Customary Law, or such law as may be introduced with the consent of the duly recognized Naga Representative Organization, save that where a sentence of transportation or death has been passed there will be right of appeal to the Governor.

   In cases arising between Nagas and non-Nagas in a) Kohima and Mokokchung Town Areas, and b) in the neighbouring plains districts, the judge, if not a Naga, will be assisted by a Naga assessor.

2. Executive: The general principle is accepted that when the Naga National Council is prepared to pay for the Naga National Council should control. This principle will apply to the work done as well as the staff employed.

   While the District Officer will be appointed at the discretion of the Governor, Sub-Division of the Naga Hills should be administered by a Sub-Divisional

Council with a full time Executive President, paid by the Naga National Council, who would be responsible to the District Officer for all matters falling within the latter's responsibility, and to the Naga National Council for matters falling within their responsibility.

In regard to:

(a) Agriculture: The Naga National Council will exercise all the powers now vested in the District Officer.

(b) P.W.D.: The Naga National Council will take over full control.

(c) Education and Forest Department: Naga National Council is prepared to pay for all the services and staff.

3. Legislature: That no laws passed by the Provincial or Central Legislature which materially affect the term of this agreement or the religious practices of the Nagas shall have legal force in the Naga Hills without the consent of the Naga National Council.

   In cases of dispute as to whether any law did so affect this agreement, the matter would be referred by the Naga National Council to the Governor who would then direct that the law in question should have no legal force in the Naga Hills pending the decision of the Central Government.

4. Land: That land with its resources in the Naga Hills should not be alienated to a non-Naga without the consent of the Naga National Council.

5. Taxation: That the Naga National Council will be responsible for the imposition, collection, and expenditure of the land revenue and house tax and of such other taxes as may be imposed by the Naga National Council.

6. Boundaries: The present administrative divisions should be modified as 1) to bring into the Naga Hills District all the forests transferred to the Sibsagar and Nowgong Districts in the past, and 2) to bring under the unified administrative unit, as far as possible, all Nagas. All the areas so included would be within the scope of the present proposed agreement. No areas should be transferred out of the Naga Hills without the consent of the Naga National Council.

7. Arms Act: The District Officer will act on the advice of the Naga National Council in accordance with the provisions of the Arms Act.

8. Regulations: The Chin Hills Regulation and Bengal Eastern Frontier Regulation will remain in force.

9. Period of Agreement: The Governor of Assam as the Agent of the Government of Indian Union will have a special responsibility for a period of ten years to ensure the due observance of this Agreement; at the end of this period, the Naga National Council will be asked whether they require the above Agreement to be extended for a further period, a new agreement regarding the future of the Naga people arrived at.

A Letter from Jail

H.F. Shri C. Rajagopalachari
Governor General of India
Government House
New Delhi

Presidency Jail, Calcutta
22 November, 1948

Your Excellency,

In the spirit of real humility, nevertheless not without a feeling of honour and glory for the sake of my country, I, A.Z. Phizo, Naga, your State Prisoner, address this letter to you as one of the spokesmen of the Naga people.

It would have been more proper if I did not have to write anything concerning myself but a prisoner always feels a certain amount of injustice, and in my case it is especially so because I have been made prisoner under peculiar circumstances which I shall deal with later on.

In the first place let me clearly state that Nagas are not hostile to Indian Union. Nagas are not anti-Indian. This explains my personal position as well, and in the land of pure democracy like Naga Hills the voice of the people is supreme. No man worth his name can say or do anything against the will of the people.

I hope your Excellency has received my previous letter of the 19th instant in which I have said that Nagas must know what India wants and India must know what the

Nagas want, to make a settlement. The unfortunate part is that the Nagas know the Indians very little and the Indians have never known the Nagas because Indians, as foreigners, were not allowed to enter into Naga country freely except on the fringes where Assam railway was made to pass through our territory touching three or four villages only. As a result we are quite strangers to one another so far. It is a new situation both of us are facing today.

Therefore let us not be impatient, but study the situation with a clear mind without scramble. In a letter of this nature I cannot touch many vital subjects of interest to which both of our two people hold an opposite view. It needs personal contact for discussion. But I write down here many things in plain language for Your Excellency to know the situation and the attitude of the Naga people.

Some interested people try to create the impression that Nagas are bent to do mischief. I want to assure Your Excellency here and now that there is no danger in Naga Hills. There is no danger in Indo-Burma border. Anybody who talks against the Nagas is not only the enemy of the Nagas but enemy to India as well. Anybody, whoever he may be, who talks as if there is danger in Indo-Burma border is a liar. Such man must have a design beyond his convincing talk. In a country where there is no police, and police was not needed, can anybody honestly believe that danger is breeding like germs in a wound?

Leaving aside other considerations, the very fact that our people do not know much about India is a positive assurance that we have no ground to go against India. There-has not yet arisen the spirit of revenge because the cause was not there for the simple reason that we have been all along living apart. We are fortunate that we do not have a traditional age-old hate to vex us which brews trouble and war.

There is another cause which eats up the confidence of men and sows seeds of discontent of one people against another. That is fear, the greatest cause of all the worries and trouble of mankind. Fear of invasion, fear of starvation by blockade, fear of economic disadvantage and exploitation. Fortunately the Naga people do not entertain the sense of fear whether of invasion or of blockade. Standing as a nation we are not worried for that. Definitely there is a distrust of economic exploitation in the fair name of development and industrialisation. And, as the possibility is of our country becoming another battlefield, the cause shall have to be eliminated.

If we look at the present problem realistically with a long view for peace and goodwill towards one another, we can see that we are living in a wonderful opportunity to bring our two people closer than ever before (I say our two people because our neighbour hill men and plains tribal people of Assam are not opposing us). We know definitely the dynamic forces latent in savagery and in civilization that create war and peace. If we refuse to eliminate the cause that creates trouble, the curse must be on us. Refusal to recognise the dangers will be like a man walking to a precipice blindfolded. So our duty is to find a way out and let good feeling come in by being reasonable before we become further estranged through inevitable consequences.

It is not the time to suspect or accuse one another. In the first place, God has made us differently to a design. Secondly we did not have the opportunity to know one another. I am quite sure that there is not a single Indian who can claim to be on friendly terms with the Naga leaders and the Nagas vice versa. Thus the situation to so-called legal implication under the cloak of Security Act or adhering to the former master's policy of 1818 Regulations will not bring the two people closer together.

The Naga people and the government of India have a constitutional difference. My detention in an Indian jail proves the contention of that difference. This also shows that the Government of India is aggressive and dangerous for the Nagas. It shows that she does not believe [in settling] differences in a democratic way through the goodwill of the people. No better proof can be given than the imprisonment of a Naga without any trial or any charge. It is an open insult to my country because your Government has arrested a spokesman while discussion for a settlement was being carried on which has not yet reached the final stage and there was no question of break in the talk on the part of the Nagas. HE the Governor of Assam will recall that on the 11th May at his house, I assured to meet him again for further talk on his proposed ten years agreement. But I still hold that my arrest against all the laws of human decency was just a tactical blunder.

Whatever it is, Naga people - and a political prisoner of a free Indian Union today as I am - [this is being expressed not through an injured feeling but] with the hope that understanding will be created. That much only is my wish.

In this transitional period of history we the Nagas are in a very delicate position. We are not minimising our responsibility in the matter of peace which is the true foundation of progress and prosperity and which confronts the whole world today. We occupy a territory at a point of transfusions and we cannot permit our Naga territory to become a political polemics. And I appeal personally to you for my countrymen that we need all the possible help and understanding so that we can contribute our share in building up a peaceful world. India can be magnanimous today.

It is not the nature of the Nagas to be secretive. And our way of stating facts plainly is sometimes misunderstood by the people of the plains. But we never made a secret of our aspiration to be independent again when the British left India. We had been active against the British occupation of our country ceaselessly. And we declared our independence on 14 August 1947.

Since we endured a life together as the British-conquered subjects along with the Indians, we sincerely believed India would not interfere in our liberty and freedom. Now, the British have left and India is politically free. But the possibility of India's annexation of Nagaland and domination over the unwilling Nagas, have become a more fearful problem than the British imperialism whose home and country was at least several thousand miles away. Day by day this appears to be nearer to a fact · than a mere possibility. We give all the praises and glory to India and particularly to Indian Congress for compelling the British to quit sooner than expected. But I hope India shall not become selfish and naughty in her greatest hour of victory. I believe both of our people do not know how to meet as we two are so [much of] strangers to one another. Still I refuse to believe that the old urge of imperialism for domination and exploitation on the name of safeguards, protection and development of the country has already gripped the heart of India within so short a time of attaining her freedom.

I do not think India has assumed that she-has inherited the "whiteman's burden" to look after the welfare of the underdeveloped people of *coloured* races against their will, but rather she has taken the lead to champion the cause of human rights. Many people in my country must be laughing secretly now, as I have been made a political hostage when I came out to Indian Union territory, because I always consider India as a peace-loving country without any aggressive design.

We shall have to take into account that materially we live in one world, but socially and politically we have not yet reach the stage where our enforced unity under one Government will make our two people loyal and friendly towards one another. Let us halt and ponder carefully.

Plainly our dilemma is how to make a settlement with India that the pride of India, in her greatest glory of achievement, can be raised up to the estimation of the world and make her feel that wonderful joy and happiness only the real giver can feel, and at the same time we free ourselves to become a distinct nation again as we were before the British conquered our country. We know as a nation from experience that a hurt feeling can never be healed. And the goodwill of India is just as important as our independence itself. We have not been careless in these matters at any time even though we are very turbulent by nature.

We wanted India to settle down more calmly so that it will not appear that we are trying to take advantage of her weakness or unsettled condition. This, we know very well, is politically dangerous. It may appear that we are very foolish. But our independence is, not a challenge. India already knew our programme which we announced publicly to the world and we never stood on pretence conducting our national affairs. Say what the critics like, we march on.

A nation standing on her birth right seeking to get back her liberty and freedom cannot be pushed aside by the march of time. So we decided to go deliberately slow. We are not swayed by passing events. We want to be considerate and careful towards others just as much as we shall have to be careful for our people. Thus we stand today respectfully but in-all humility to face you in a friendly way. Real peace can be created and preserved only through mutual respect and understanding. I still consider that we are following the right policy.

The question of the finalisation of the Indian Constitution was there. And we felt that it was our duty to restate and inform the Indian Union again of our decision to remain independent even though she had already been informed. It was not because we have declared our independence and so we mean to stick to it, but it was and it has been the wish of the people to remain independent.

Our wish was made known to Mr. Attlee, the present Prime Minister of England. When his party came to Kohima, Naga Hills, with Sir John Simon Commission in 1929, it was noted. As a result, we were kept in the "Excluded Area." It may be added here that the Nagas are not legal minded and mere legalistic argument is considered trivial and immoral. Simply because once we were chained together in our slavery, we hope that that period of our misfortune shall not form the important point of historical sequence for our two people to quarrel at any time. We must settle our own affairs amicably.

Propaganda was made for a long time in the Indian Press by interested people accusing the Nagas in one way or another. We kept quite. We have been accused to be in league with the British and Americans or someone else. So I shall mention briefly the diverse problems we had to face in overcoming many difficulties some of which I can mention now for the first time.

Problem 1

Our immediate problem was to fight against a colonial scheme. It was well known to Indian leaders that the British wanted to establish a colony known as North Eastern Agency. The best brains of the Nagas were wholeheartedly with the British in the scheme. That was part of their spontaneous loyalty. The British could have easily got 190,000 sq. miles or more and colonise it—protest or no protest. It was not difficult for them to get even 200,000sq miles because much more than that were in a fluid state with the people entirely pro-British in their attitude. This may appear to be fantastic but a careful study of the area will show the possibility of maintaining two parts. One in Manngdow-Buthidannj region with Chittagong to be a free port-for some time as the British cannot think of a state without an outlet of seaport. Then, the other one is the Moulmein - Tavoy region of seaport. Then, the other one is the Moulmein - Tavoy region to the sea where the well-known Ioyal British-made Karens predominate with Mons and other hill people. Above Tenesarim division there are Shans in the Shan states, then Chins and Kachins with the Karens who form the best soldiers in Burma and who were very loyal to the British. They would choose living in a British colony than in an independent Burma. In Upper Burma the portion towards Myitkyina region of Hukong-Mogok Valley, then towards Assam through Naga territory including Kabaw Valley with Manipur State (two thirds of the state belongs to the hillmen), then Lushai Hills down to Chittagong Hill Tracts of Maungdaw-Buthidannj region to the sea. Further up towards Sadiya there are Abors, Miris and Mishmis and Tirap frontier. All this, if it were made a reality with full support of the hill people could have become a state of some importance from the very day of its birth without having to worry about any internal disturbances from the very inception as people have a brotherly feeling towards one another.

The idea was, I am sure, hatched by Naga Hills Administrators who were always clever and stout-hearted British aristocrats. But without the support and full cooperation of the Naga Leaders it could not be materialised. If the scheme was allowed to take shape only Brahmaputra Valley might have been left to Assarn because Silchar plains would have gone to Pakistan and Khasis and Garo

Hills might have joined the federation of a very strong hill people's state even though the name would be colony.

Was it a feasible scheme? In Assam, Digboi oil-field and coal fields could belong to the colony. Hill people and plain tribals could easily fight it out. Patheria Test oil deposits might be taken over on approval. In Burma area, the iron ore mines at Nawnghkio in the northern Shan States, Wolfram and lead at Mawehi mines, Tavoy tin mines, amber and jades in Hukong valley would belong to the colony because these contiguous geographical regions belong to a people of same attitude with fraternal feelings of non-Burmese stock. They like the British and would have fallen into any British scheme. Assam plains might have joined the federation voluntarily especially when communication with Indian Union became a real problem. The Assamese people are friendly with the hill men and economically it would be to their advantage.

The colony would have become a master stroke for a few cunning British schemers with a people on their side who are more loyal to them than they expect from even their own people in England..... Even if Burma portion failed to materialise, Assam hills frontier alone could have formed a state with British brain and capital behind it and the area as big as the whole of Bengal with a seaport facility and population over three million people.

Naga leaders stood against the scheme of colony because it would go against the interest of other Eastern people. We could go down in history as a people who stood against freedom of the East, besides we wanted to manage our own country independently without interference in any form. We had to fight against the scheme for a long time and the better part of our leaders' time was exhausted before the transfer of power took place.

When the last British Governor of Assam visited Naga Hills in Mokokchung, his speech was directed against our stand in tone of insult in pious exhortation denouncing the Naga independence struggle. But we know better. We had won.

Before the power was actually transferred there was not much time left to us to come into contact with Indian leaders. Another barrier was that we did not know one another, besides; the remnant British officials became hostile towards the Nagas. The mischief they created prior to their departure remains wholly uncured upto now. Anyhow we have not failed the Eastern people in the fight and struggle against British imperialism.

Problem No. 2: Home Front

Without a strong foundation at home there can be no unity and no peace. After we successfully fought against the British scheme we had to face our home front. I do not know whether it was known to India that the British mischievously advised the Nagas to remain within India saying that India would be broken up into pieces within five years. And they refused to pay the salary of those government servants who stood for Naga independence. They were threatened with imprisonment and fine. As a result Government servants started quarreling with the British remnant officials and the internal situation of our country was badly disturbed.

We did not wart chaos and we had to rearrange the whole organisation in the country. We wanted the, Government servant to remain in their respective posts, all of them. So they had to resign from our NCC and other regional committees whatever they might be as they were given the leading part in the British time.'

The village panchayats, and Group and Regional committees were mostly in the hands of the people in the villages all the time. In the organisation there was not a single village which was not represented. Even then it took up a lot of time to rearrange on the whole-country basis. And as our people were cultivators we always move with the season. So we take a long time to decide important issues.

There was a time when a certain outside element got into internal politics. During those days one so-called "ultimatum" was given to India by wholly unwarranted and unauthorised persons without consulting the people. Without the approval the people first, our country never recognises anything. But we owe an apology.

To eradicate the whole undesirable elements without creating unnecessary commotion, a slow process to get rid of them without shouting was found desirable. The whole thing fizzled out. But we felt another setback for some time. In the land of democracy, people are undemonstrative. We live in peaceful obscurity. Events do not move fast. That is another reason why you will have to have patience to come to know the Naga people.

Our Problem No.3: Final Stage

Whatever the Nagas want, the decision is left with the people and no man can individually do much. Unless some radical change has taken place within the last five months (July onward) after my arrest we have come to the last stage of settling our affair with India. And I want to make my position quite clear to Your Excellency. It is important for myself and for my country.

As a spokesman I can only say what my people want and what they have decided. Nothing less but nothing more. Besides that final say is with the people. Our country is so organised that no man all can pretend to speak for the people unless he knows the whole situation, or he is authorised. The position of a spokesman and a loader is often confused. And I want to believe that my arrest was due to such a misjudgement. A leader of an organisation may be able to shout and say many things but not a spokesman. Like a pilot the spokesman shall have to follow a direction.

To settle a difference it needs the parties to meet face to face. After coming to know one another, in the middle of negotiation, if one party is to kidnap away the spokesman of the other party in this fashion as their political hostage, the talk cannot be carried on. If any settlement is made through threat or trickery it cannot be accepted and recognised.

The way I have been arrested under a legal pretext can have no excuse and no country will tolerate for long this sort of insult. Leaving aside Gandhiji's principle which is being outraged every day, my detention is an open violation of the very principle of non-cooperation for which the Congress of India is supposed to stand.

HE the Governor of Assam, Sir Akbar Hydari has been mostly responsible for the present controversy between the Nagas and India from June 1947 and onward. Otherwise something should have been known even if time were to be taken for India to settle down more calmly.

In February 1947, Naga people demanded of H M Government and/ or the Government of India an Interim Government for a period of 10 years. When the subcommittee of the Constituent assembly of India came to Kohima we could not carryon any discussion because they wanted the Nagas to be within India whereas the final aim of the Nagas has all along been Independence without any foreign interference, whoever that may be.

Many unexpected things happen in the march of History, so our experience was not the exception. Knowing that the subcommittee mission was a failure, HE the Governor of Assam, Sir Akbar Hydari came to Kohima with his Secretary and Adviser Mr Adams, a former British official in Naga Hills for years who acted as DC in Kohima for some time. He was one of the men who told the Nagas to remain with India saying that India would go to pieces within five years. So the Nagas could get out any time as if we would like to be glorified through someone's downfall. It is much to be regretted that for settlement of national affairs people do not entertain a healthy idea on the basis of mutual understanding and agreement.

The proposed agreement, better known as "Governor's ten years agreement", based on the Interim Government for ten years demanded by the Nagas in February 1947, was fully discussed. At that time four-fifths of the members of the NNC were Government servants. It was in June 1947 under duress of official high pressure that NNC was divided, Sir Pawsey, the last British DC was there then. As most of the NNC members were Government servants, it was made to be considered as accepted. During the discussion of the Agreement Sir Akbar Hydari threatened the Nagas with military power. The Naga public rejected Sir Akbar Hydari's agreement. His threat was considered as a challenge and it enraged the people. On his return from Imphal, Manipur State, he was informed by the people in writing. As a spokesman I am in a difficult position. I cannot displease the one to please the other. I hope India will come to know Naga people better.

Unless people in my country have taken another course the "Governor's ten-year agreement" will, I believe, form the basis of an agreement. But the Indian Government must be perfectly sincere and honest with the Nagas in their discussion and in their dealings. There will be no honour to deceive or cheat a small people like the Nagas. India must consider the position of the Nagas and compare with her own position of the past. If India once felt the weight of domination of people who were 4,000 miles away, whose people were seven times smaller than her own population, from a country twenty times smaller than India itself, the Nagas will feel the weight of the connection with India like a rat under the foot of an elephant. Some other people on the border joining the Indian Union voluntarily must not form the basis of consideration.

To entertain the idea that an agreement cannot be reached satisfactorily of this State is either a lie or an outright greediness. To settle the present difference it is not a question of the people but a settlement of land that belongs to the Nagas.

It is a criminal habit to talk in terms of military expedition when a satisfactory settlement cannot be reached. But even that much question does not arise tin our case. The land that will form the basis of settlement entirely belongs to the Nagas. When I hear the leaders talk about fighting for settlement of a difference, I always wonder if such men had gone through the experience of butchering mankind. Vain glory and cowardly leadership often let loose carnage and destroy all the basis of understanding when they do not know what more to do.

It is mean to take advantage of another man's weakness. During the transitional period of transfer of power when India was quite helpless we never contemplated to take advantage of such a weak situation. I always entertain the hope that one Eastern race (especially those who got back their freedom from their white master) will not attempt to dominate another people. No other nation had a better experience than India to lead the world to freedom from the course of imperialism and domination. It is for India to show the way out.

Till now I do not know why I have been imprisoned. I suspect that Sir Akbar Hydari does not want me to be a spokesman of my people because I pointed out the flaws in his "Agreement." Whatever the outcome may be, it is not me but my people who have the final say.

As for Sir Akbar Hydari, we hold the opinion that he was not a sincere man and he had a double motive trying to create such a situation in a peaceful country like ours. This I have very plainly stated to the DCSB office in my statement. Also, I have told all what SB wanted to know because the Nagas have nothing to hide and our independence is not a secret to be hidden. On the other hand, to become suspicious or get frightened with the facts is cowardly.

What would be inevitable shall have to be faced. The earlier it is done the better. For the first time in our history the Naga people have witnessed the greatest provocation. In ordinary times it would not have been tolerated. Innocent Naga women have been fired at and molested. This was committed by Indian Union soldiers. Three men were shot dead in cold blood in a village. The hated British had not done this sort of things even when they conquered our country. They fought a fair fight without shooting men in cold blood and they never molested women. Even in the last war when the Japanese overran our country there was not a single case where women were molested by the terrible Japanese soldiers but Indian soldiers had a black record to their sorrow. Sir Akbar Hydari had given a sample of his threat and I sent him a message to the effect that "so now you have let the cat out, All-ho-Akbar." I am certain about one thing-s-my turbulent Naga people cannot be frightened into submission.

If India wants to shoot, the Nagas shall face the bullets without retaliation as much as humanly possible. We shall refuse to submit to evil things. We shall not barter our birth right freedom, liberty and independence to the enemy bullet. And we shall not start fighting with India and give her a chance to put our country under military control in the name of internal trouble. Sir Akbar Hydari's double scheme is dangerous both for the Nagas and the Indian Union. As for our case it will be settled by all means without a fight. Our case is absolutely clear, and we stand appealing for sanity.

For us it is not a matter to feel ashamed about to say that we are backward in many respects. But it will not be a credit to India, the champion of the freedom of mankind, if India will try to twist and turn a situation through a certain legal flaw and take possession of Naga Lands against the will of people. If India thinks that she had a line on Naga Hills through the British Bill of Independence, nothing hinders India from becoming a benevolent giver now.

The Naga people are good administrators and we live under a system of pure democracy. We are capable of managing our country without having anything to worry or fear. Our people have gone so far as to say that if India cannot or will not supply anything, we shall not complain and we shall not protest. If we cannot stand on our own feet there is no meaning in talk of independence.

How we conduct our affairs may not be known to Indians as we are so little known. We have Chiefs in many places but no Chief can do things against the will of the people. They are not feudal Chiefs but only head of the people. All villages are under Panchayat system of its own and they are quite independent having nothing to worry about interference in all the internal matters.

Every Naga family has got its own house and lands for cultivation. No family needs worry for land. The land belongs to the people forming mostly individual property. We never pay land tax and we never paid tax to the British. The feeling of personal ownership with perfect liberty is ingrained in the life of our people. As a result our nature hungers after absolute freedom.

Psychologically this form of existence has much to do with our national struggle to remain independent without interference. To the Nagas independence is a desire.

No man is so rich (not even the Chiefs) nor any family is so poor as to worry for the next month. No man possesses so much land depriving others, such a practice the community shall not allow. The shrewd British never interfered with the people, not even their land. Arrest was something unknown. Police was not necessary and only about thirty police used to be kept for traffic duty in Kohima town. The people were left alone and perfectly free, but no improvement was encouraged. As a result socially and economically Nagas remain the same today as we were hundreds of years ago. But this is not something to be regretted. Our apparent backwardness is an asset to us. We start our new life on virgin soil with modern plans.

It was known to India that the Nagas have never been very quiet under the British even before the last war. When war came, and our country became the scene of a terrible battlefield, the spirit of adventure for many found an outlet. To many it was a thrill with modern weapons. But the war also changed the mind of our people. It does not pay to fight other men's war and war is to be avoided if at all possible. So the bitter experience we passed through will not be all a loss to our future generations.

Leaving aside the question of advantages and disadvantages, people felt a deeper need, an experience which scarcely visits a country like a rare comet. People have seen independence in the darkness of war like the beautiful starry world which can be seen only in the darkness of the night. Peace was heard in the thundering sound of bombs and cannons. The meaning of defence can be realised only on a battlefield. The people who value life in higher conception and who lived in the war shattered country have seen independence more clearly than anybody can paint a picture. All is like a vision that can never be forgotten. Will any sensible man like to leave even a remote chance for his children to live on the battlefield again?

I can only repeat once again that it is unfortunate that Indian do not know us and we did not know the Indian leaders before. But then we never made any secret about our determination to be independent regardless of the consequences an independent country had to face. I believe with my countrymen that the chord of bondage that kept our two people tied together in slavery having been cut off, we shall be able to trust one another better in our freedom as equals. Our relationship will grow spontaneously through new understanding and mutual trust.

As a small nation you can trust us. As a big nation we shall have confidence in you.

In conclusion let me enumerate briefly that:

(a) There is no secret and no danger in Naga Hills.

(b) The final say is with the people and not with a particular individual.

(c) The Nagas are not planning Machiavellian politics.

(d) The consideration of balancing a power or seeking a strong partnership is out or-question.

(e) The Naga people are not against the Indian Union.

(f) The Governor's "Ten Year Agreement" based on Naga demand or any other agreement must be settled in a constitutional manner without any show of force or coercion or trickery.

(g) I must be released or tried in a law court of justice.

(h) Freedom, liberty and peace are the first and the last consideration.

(i) The Nagas stand for sanity appealing to you for an understanding.

Finally, let me say that our stand was not through pure selfishness of gain or glory. It was something deeper than that. Situated as we are, surrounded by the biggest nations in the world like India on one hand in the west, on the other hand China in the northeast, and a most determined people like the Burmese in the east and Pakistan further south and then, still further of a people towards north whose future destiny is still in the balance who are racially Tibeto-Mongolian with a geographical contiguity towards the east rather than towards the west, placed as we are in such a situation, we cannot ignore existing facts and overlook remote possibilities. So we have a special responsibility to consider the welfare of our future generations and for maintaining tranquility for a lasting peace where we have been sandwiched in an inextricable position with diverse nations on all sides.

The Nagas were divided by the British administration into three major units. About one-fifth of Naga population with that much in proportion of our land were administered from British India. About the same proportion was administered by British Burma. And approximately sixty per cent of the population occupying a territory of about seventy percent of Nagaland were left untouched and undisturbed who were absolutely independent having no homage to pay to other country and no country has the right to encroach on their territory.

Nagaland is a compact geographical unit with clearly demarcated boundaries before the advent of the British. The boundaries that were shifted after British occupation for administrative convenience were officially recorded.

I hope on careful consideration, the inevitable position we occupy will be appreciated. It is not through irresponsible isolationism or foolishness or with an evil motive of aggression for which we have been struggling to regain our independence for the last seventy years, ever since we were conquered. The first attempt was made within three months, and in the very first year of surrender we besieged the British forces on two occasions but help and reinforcement were always available from Indian soil.

With the rest of the Eastern people you also hated imperialism whether white or brown. All the Eastern people were on in that. We all stood against and fought like one man. I hope the Eastern free nations shall not try to dominate again their weaker sister nations in any form against their will. Lf such policy be pursued there can be no happiness in this world.

Representation to the President of India by the Kilonsers on Behalf of the Free Nagaland on 18th September 1954

To, September 18, 1954

The President,
Republic of India,
New Delhi, India.

Your Excellency,

In the manner of the Naga administering their Country, the Government of the People's Sovereign Republic of free Nagaland is composed of the following KILONSERS (Administering Elders):

1. Hongkin
2. Khoni
3. Lokokmong
4. Meshe
5. Pangba
6. Pohsha
7. Pomong

8. Sakobomong
9. Shonyimong
10. Shamnyak
11. Tomukam
12. Ungbok
13. Yemba
14. Yemba

The above mentioned KILONSERS, on behalf of Free Nagaland bring this representation to your Excellency.

The Indian treat the free Nagas as their subject and much more like slaves. It must be clearly understood that Free Nagas had never been anybody's subject in History.

The influence of Mahatma Gandhi was so great that the people of Free Nagaland had been calmly tolerating the Indian troops for all these years hoping that the truth will ultimately prevail. Regardless of how the free Indians misbehaved towards the Nagas, our people never retaliated nor did they attempt even to defend themselves. Since the doctrine of non-violence is now fast running our front the Indian Government officers and troops alike, "Ahimsa" has become a mockery, and the Free Naga people have no more patience left just to stand and see the Indian Officers and troops shooting our people and beating, slapping and kicking as if we are their slaves. Women are being so often molested and raped that the depravity and lustfulness of the Indians now is Free Nagaland would certainly put you to shame and the Indian Nation as a whole.

The unbearable circumstance precipitated by the Indian troops again and again made it imperative on the part of the Free Naga people to raise their long suppressed voice now to say that the Indians and the Nagas can never live together as friends, in an atmosphere of peace, which is very necessary for human progress and happiness.

As a free and matured nation, we waited patiently bearing our untold woes and trouble expecting Justice from India. Such torture and insult never experienced in our History before, is now let loose on us, peace loving people.

We believe your Excellency have never been told by anybody that the Nagas of free Nagaland have had an uninterrupted traditional history of 1700 years, as a free and Independent Nation and no Foreign Nation had ever always been a Democratic People and a change or ruling cliques had never known to us. Our forefathers were always true and friendly to our neighbours around us.

In 1880, the British challenged our Sovereignty and we successfully defended our Country is the proof of our conscious effort to keep alive as a separate and distinct nation which had not undergone any metamorphosis for a greater or wider nationality. And we know what we are not too proud to say this.

We have been so warned that we do not know where and when your troops will attack our people. Sudden raiding of villages becomes such a constant incident that is no more new to us. Our Country is already in a stage of anarchy as a result of your necked aggression. We hereby earnestly appeal to your honour for immediate withdrawal of your Army and leave us as before.

This is the first note ever written and submitted to your Government Naga traditional courtesy demands personal discussion for serious matters of this kind, confronting our nation today, but our representatives so often got beaten, whenever they approached Indian Political Officers, as such personal contact became impossible. And hence we submit our case to you for your consideration and necessary action.

1. Our people are being killed for no reason.
2. Many people have been tortured and beaten to death.
3. Women are raped and often molested that women fell unsafe wherever there are Indians.
4. Our fields were destroyed and houses burnt down.
5. Our woodland and forest were cut down just to arouse us to anger.
6. Our houses are being raided day and night, insulting men and women.
7. The houses belonging to our national leaders had been set on fire and the chiefs are often slapped, kicked and beat.
8. Lands are being demanded on pain of death, for Air base.
9. The troops are hunting the leaders and elders of our country, as if they are wild animal, roaming in the field, in the jungles and in the rivers and the people are being blindly fired upon as such there is no security for human life.

Now where is the "Human Rights' for us Nagas? To where shall our people go, to the sky above or underneath the earth? The Hon'ble Prime Minister of India, Jawaharlal Nehru, said, "Human being ultimately counts," Are not the Nagas also human beings? How can we live in peace when we are under constant threat and molestation? Do the Indians want the Nagas extinct?

How the Indians behave in Nagaland? They say, "We have come to help you. We are not here to collect taxes from you". Is it a fact? Leave us alone.

This is the stock phrase of every Indian officer. Their words and their actions never go well together. On September 14,

1954, the Indian political officer called the people of Noklak Village (500) to get together and he demanded a big area of land for a Military base, and at the same time he warned the people that the village would be wiped away if they refused to yield to his demand. The same officers sent out troops and broadcast a proclamation that all the Chiefs of various villages must come and meet him with presents, such as goats, fowls, eggs, natives' costumes spears and duos. Those Chiefs whoever failed to come were to be severely dealt with. But nobody went to see him and the political officers sent out 20 soldiers to Yakum Village (140 houses) and the houses of the Two Chiefs were destroyed and six people were seriously injured. This was "to teach a lesson".

On July 7, 1954, a political officer sent his troops to Chingmei Village (160) houses and they killed some of the people. 31 people escaped with bullet injuries. Later on the village was asked to enter into a pledge not to wage war with Indians and it was done so. The village was threatened once again by another political officer for whom a letter was send addressing him. Another political officer, reported to be a Police officer from Bombay, also passed through the same village and called the Village Elders and the Pastor of the said village. The Pastor went first and he was kicked, slapped and beaten for a long time by the political officers himself, who was kept bound and he ordered the soldiers to torture him. When the soldiers were on the way, the servant of the political officer saved them and had made them run away. He was later beaten. The order was given to shoot the elders down and the soldiers had taken position to fire. This incident took place on September 9, 1954, and the Pastor is still in the custody of the political officer. Men like this officer can easily create hatred, enmity and bloodshed wherever they go.

Those are only few examples, just to show you what atmosphere the Free Nagas are now being compelled to live in. More than 500 of our people have already been perished.

In few Nagaland, Indian Government follows a systematic policy of beating and torturing whenever they can lay hands on any Naga. An Indian officer told the Nagas in 1952 that Nagas are to live as Indian coolies but actually we are being treated more than slaves. A political officer now warns than 14 or 15 villages will be wiped out" to bring the Nagas to their senses, to behave properly.

We know that preparation have been going on for what they call "a large scale drive" by air and by land. Any moment anything may happen. Our people were compelled to go back to the primordial days of old, and defend themselves or die in the hands of Indians for the honour of our country and for our Naga nation. India can take our land but not our people.

If the Nagas say they are an independent nation, they must be prepared to defend themselves where and when they are attacked. That is Logical. Every Independent nation would react in the same way. But we are too small and too weak a Nation to stand ourselves.

We do not want anything from India. We do not yearn for peace after much bloodshed. PLEASE LEAVE US ALONE. Indian officer told us again and again that Indian has 10 lakhs soldiers to fight with a tiny backward nation like the Free Nagas. Blood is being shed and more blood is likely to shed and the same would simply widen the gulf between Nagas and Indians. Now we are prepared to die then to submit.

So, we, on behalf of our Sovereign Republic of Free Nagaland, and on behalf of our Free Nagas, do hereby humbly and most respectfully request your Excellency's Government to withdraw the Indian troops honourably from our Free Nagaland. We are stating these things hoping a favourable reply from your government.

(SEAL)
Kautaga
Free Nagaland

Your
Signed/- Hongkhin
For KILONSERS
Government of Free NAGALAN

The 16-Point Agreement Arrived at Between the Government of India and the Naga People's Convention, July, 1960

1. **The Name:** The territories that were therefore known as the Naga Hills-Tuensang Area under the Naga Hills - Tuensang Area Act, 1957, shall form a State within the Indian Union and be hereafter known as Nagaland.

2. **The Ministry Incharge:** The Nagaland shall be under the Ministry of External Affairs of the Government of India.

3. **The Governor of Nagaland:**

   (a) The President of India shall appoint a Governor for Nagaland and he will be vested with the executive powers of the Government to Nagaland. He will have his headquarters in Nagaland.

   (b) His administrative secretariat will be headed by the Chief Secretary stationed at the Headquarters with other Secretariat staff as necessary.

   (c) The Governor shall have special responsibility with regard to law and order during transitional period and for so long as the law and order situation continues remain disturbed on account of hostile activities. In exercising this special responsibility, the Governor shall, after consultation with the Ministry, act in his individual judgment. This special responsibility of the Governor will cease when normalcy returns.

4. **Council of Ministers:**

   (a) There shall be a Council of Ministers with a Chief Minister at the head to assist and advise the Governor in the exercise of his functions.

   (b) The council of Ministers shall be responsible to the Naga Legislative Assembly.

5. **The Legislature:** There shall be constituted a Legislative Assembly consisting of elected and nominated members as may be deemed necessary representing different tribes. (Further a duly constituted body of Export may be formed to examine and determine the principles of representation on democratic basis).

6. **Representation in the Parliament:** Two elected members shall represent Nagaland in the Union Parliament, that it to say, one for the Lok Sabha and the other for the Rajya Sabha.

7. **Acts of Parliament:** No act or law passed by the Union Parliament affecting the following provisions shall have legal force in the Nagaland unless specifically applied to it by a majority vote of the Nagaland Legislative Assembly:

   (a) The Religious or Social Practices of the Nagas.

   (b) The Customary Laws and Procedure.

   (c) Civil and Criminal Justice so far as these concern decision according to the Naga Customary Law.

   The existing law relating to administration of

civil and criminal justice as provided in the Rules for the Administration of Justice and Police in the Naga Hills District shall continue to be in force.

(d) The ownership and transfer of land and its resources.

8. **Local Self-Government:** Each tribe shall have the following units of rule making and administrative local bodies to deal with matters concerning the respective tribes and areas:

(a) The Village Council;

(b) The Range Council; and

(c) The Tribal Council.

The council will also deal with disputes and cases involving breaches of customary laws and usages.

9. **Administration of Justice:**

(a) The existing system of administration of civil and criminal justice shall continue.

(b) Appellate courts:

(i) The District Court-cum-Session Court (for each district), High Court and Supreme Court of India;

(ii) The Naga Tribunal (for the whole Nagaland) in respect of cases decided according to Customary Law.

10. **Administration of the Tuengsang District:**

(a) The Governor shall carry on the administration of the Tuensang District for a period of 10 (ten) years until such time when the tribes in the Tuengsang District are capable of shouldering more responsibility of advance system of administration in other parts of the Nagaland

(b) Provided further that a regional Council shall be formed for Tuengsang District by representatives from all the tribes in Tuengsang District, and the Governor may nominate representative to the Regional Council as well. The Regional Council will elect Member of the Naga Legislative Assembly to represent Tuengsang District.

(c) Provided further that on the advice of the Regional Council steps will be taken to start various Councils and Courts, in those areas where the people feel themselves capable of establishing such institutions.

(d) Provided further that the no Act or Law passed by the Legislative Assembly shall be applicable to Tuensang District unless specially recommended by the Regional Council.

(e) Provided further that the Regional Council shall supervise and guide the working of the various Councils and Tribal Courts within Tuensang District wherever necessary and depute the local officers to act as Chairmen thereof.

(f) Provided further that Councils of such areas inhabited by a mixed population or which have not as yet decided to which specific Tribal Council be affiliated to, shall be directly under the Regional Council for the time being. And at the end often years the situation will be reviewed and if the people so desired the period will be further extended.

11. **Financial Assistance from the Government of India:** To supplement the revenues of Nagaland, there will be need for the Government of India to payout of the consolidated Fund of Nagaland, and a grant-in aid

towards meeting the cost of administration. Proposals for the above grants shall be prepared and submitted by the Government of Nagaland to the Government of India for their approval. The Governor will have general responsibility for ensuring that the funds made available by the Government of India are expended for the purposes for which they have been approved.

12. **Consolidation of Forest Areas:** The delegation wished the following to be placed on record: "The Naga delegation discussed the question of the inclusion of the Reserve Forests and of contiguous areas inhabited by the Nagas. They were referred to the provisions in Articles 3 and 4 of the Constitution, prescribing the procedure for the transfer of areas from one state to another".

13. **Consolidation of Contiguous Naga Areas:** The delegation wished the following to be passed on record: "The Naga leaders expressed the view that other Nagas inhabiting contiguous areas should be enabled to join the new state. It was pointed out to them on behalf of the Government of India that Articles 3 and 4 of the Constitution provided for increasing the areas of any state, but it was possible for the Government of India to make any commitment in this regard at this stage".

14. **Formation of Separate Naga Regiment:** In order that the Naga people can fulfill their desire of playing a full role in the defense forces of India, the question of raising a separate Naga Regiment should be duly examine for action.

15. **Transitional Period:**

    (a) On reaching the political settlement with the government of India, the government of India will prepare a Bill for such amendment of the

Constitution, as may be necessary, in order to implement the decision. The draft Bill, before presentation to Parliament, will be shown to the delegates of the N.P.C.

(b) There shall be constituted an Interim Body with elected representatives from every tribe, to assist and advice the Governor in the administrative of Nagaland during the transitional period. The tenure of office of the members of the Interim Body will be 3 (three) years subject to the re-election.

16. **Inner Line Regulation:** Rules embodied in the Bengal Eastern frontier Regulation, 1973, shall remain in force in Nagaland.

Cease Fire in Nagaland (6Th September, 1964)

Terms of Agreement for Cease Fire of Cessation of Hostilities in Nagaland.

1. In hope of bringing about a Cease Fire or cessation of hostilities and a peaceful settlement, we the undersigned appointed members of the Federal Government of Nagaland have given serious consideration to the terms of an agreement designed to bring about a Cease Fire throughout Nagaland for the purpose of enabling a Peace Conference to be held and consultations to take place freely among the people of Nagaland and India.

2. On the understanding that the terms communicated to us by the Peace Mission and now clarified on a number of points after consultation With both sides will constitute an agreement with the Government of India with whom the negotiations for a lasting peace settlement will take place; we agree on behalf of the Federal Government of Nagaland as from a date to be decided to suspend all forms of violent activities.

3. On the understanding that the Security Forces of the Government of India undertake to suspend:

   (a) Jungle operation;

(b) Raiding of Federal Army and Federal administrative camps.

(c) Patrolling beyond 1,000 yards of Security post.

(d) Searching of villages;

(e) Aerial action;

(f) Arrest;

(g) Imposition of forced labour; and

(h) Imposition of political fines.

4. We, on behalf of the Government of Nagaland also undertake to suspend:

(a) Sniping and ambushing;

(b) Imposition of fines;

(c) Kidnapping and recruitment;

(d) Sabotage activities;

(e) Raiding and firing at Security posts, towns and administrative centres; and

(f) Moving with arms in towns, villages and administrative centres; wherever there are Security posts and approaching within 1,000 yards of the Security Post.

5. Since the above terms will make it possible for members of Federal Government and Naga Army to move about freely and to hold necessary consultations with the people in an atmosphere of calm and freedom from tension, we also give assurance that Federal Army personal will refrain from moving with arms and in uniform in towns and villages and within a radius of one thousand yards of Security posts. We undertake that special arrangements may be made in cases where movement with arms and in uniforms

become necessary in any area where there may be risk of encounter with Security Forces, e.g. along or across roads or bridges.

6. The understanding given by both sides should preclude an unexpected encounter but in the event of any such encounter ever occurring between Federal Government personal and security Forces the rule “no firing unless first fired upon” will be strictly observed during the “Cease Fire” period.

7. On our part also, we undertake to promote an atmosphere conducive to peaceful occupations and free discussion, not to use the period of the “Cease Fire” to parade with arms in inhabited areas from which the Security Forces are precluded by this agreement.

8. In the International Border area, Security Forces will maintain patrolling to a depth on miles as the crow flies from the frontier line. In this particular matter arrangement can be made for further modification when Cease Fire is affected.

9. We also give the assurance that no arms will be imported from abroad by the Federal Government of Nagaland during the period of Cease Fire.

10. As a first step, the proposed period of Cease Fire or cessation of hostilities will be declares for one month from an agreed date after allowing 15 days from the time this agreement is reached to enable all concerned to be informed of the terms and conditions of the Cease Fire of cessation of hostilities.

11. The Government of India during the period of Cease Fire will continue the protection of Army convoys on maintenance service; and the usual road patrolling; in the connection will extent to not more than 100 yards on either side of the road. The road patrols will

withdraw when the convoy has passed. The Federal Army personal shall move about freely when the convoys passed The Federal Army personal shall move about freely when the convoys passed the locality, and also in non-convoy days. The days of the week and the particulars of route used by the convoys will be notified in advance and communicated to the Federal Government.

12. That a peace talk shall take place after the Cease Fire period is declared. The peace talk is between the Federal Government of Nagaland and the Government of India. The Government of India can bring any number of delegates at the peace talk that shall represent the Government of India.

13. The above terms will apply throughout Nagaland.

Dated Oking — Signed on behalf of the Federal
10th August, 1964 — Government of Nagaland

1. Zashei Huire
   Ahng, Japfu State,
2. Biseto Medom,
   Lota-Kilonser,
3. L.Z. Zhenito,
   Tatar, Federal Government of Nagaland

Nagaland Peace Mission's Proposals

During the recess, after the ninth round of Indo-Naga Peace Talks, the Nagaland Peace Mission came forward with a new proposal on 20 December 1964 for consideration of both Indian and Naga delegation. The proposal reads:

1. It has been a matter of considerable satisfaction to the Peace Mission, as to all others in Nagaland and in the rest of India that since firing ceased on 6 September 1964, for the first time in ten years people in Nagaland are experiencing what normalcy is. The Peace Mission feels that it is the moral obligation of everyone in Nagaland and, more so, of the Peace Mission, in which so much confidence and faith have been reposed, to see that this peace becomes everlasting in Nagaland. It is in pursuance of this that the Peace Mission is addressing this communication to both the parties.

2. But first it should be placed on records to the honour of both parties that are in conflict that the attempt to find peace and agreement to a cease-fire was an adventurous step which issued from their deep desire to find an honourable way to terminate such a bitter, wasteful and protracted conflict.

3. The marked difference in the atmosphere that prevails in Nagaland today as compared with the prevailing

prior to the cessation of operation will probably be only realized by those who have lived or worked in Nagaland where there was, as soon as darkness began, a sense of insecurity resulting from the ever present possibility of sudden violence. Today, the people are returning to their normal occupations. Families are being reunited, the biggest harvest for many years has been gathered and there is a feeling of hope in Nagaland which makes every delegate engage in the peace talks only too conscious of the heavy burden of decision on those who have to take it, the life and happiness of so many human beings being dependent on the decisions that are taken. In all this, it is fair to pay tributes not only to the Government of India for their humanity and imagination, but also to the leaders of the Baptist Church for whom this initiative was the result of much thought and powerful consideration of the good of both India and Nagaland.

4. The Nagaland Peace Talks, which started on 23 September 1964, have now come to a stage, where the NFG Delegation have placed their demands for consideration by the Government of India. This was in response to the statement of the leader of the Government of India delegation of Chedema on 14 November, wherein the Government of India also stated their position and understanding of the problem, as they saw it.

6. The Nagaland Federal Delegation have claimed that Nagaland had never been conquered by the Indian Army or ruled by an Indian Government, although their territory had been forcibly annexed by the British Army and the British Government about a century ago. Nevertheless, their right of self-determination they claim belonged to them separately as a people from

the Sovereign Independent-State of India, and they are now demanding recognition of this Independence which, they say, India herself demanded and heroically struggled for under the historic slogan of "Swaraj".

7. The Government of India's position on the other hand, is that Nagaland formed an integral part of India before 1947 and that, with the transfer of power to India by the British Parliament, Nagaland became a part of India in the same way as all other States in India. At the same time, the Government of India claim that they already accepted the need for granting the fullest autonomy to Nagaland by constituting the State of Nagaland so as to ensure the fullest development of the Nagas and to guarantee their separate ethnic and cultural entity and to ensure their traditional right and their resources accordingly; the Nagas are not ruled by any alien power but are ruling themselves.

8. The Peace Mission notes that a section of the Naga people accepted the status of statehood thus conferred upon Nagaland as being in their best interest. Another section did not consider that if satisfied the aims and objectives they had been fighting for. Thus, there are these two divergent positions of the Government of India and the NFG confronting each other.

9. Though the two positions appear to be far apart, the Peace Mission believes that, with goodwill and understanding on both sides, a solution acceptable to both can be found.

10. As earlier stated, the Peace Mission reiterates that it is under an inescapable obligation to ensure maintenance of peace and settlement of all outstanding problems through peaceful means. The Peace Mission believes that there is no human problem that cannot be solved

by peaceful means. The Peace Mission further believes that the Governments concerned and the people concerned share and subscribe to this view.

11. While the Peace Mission fully agrees and endorses the principle that all subject peoples have the right to self-determination and that no group of people is competent to rule over another, it also has to invite the attention of the Nagaland Federal Government to certain historical processes that had taken place to give birth to the Union of India and to the emergence of the great concepts and ideals underlying the Union Constitution.

12. The British had conquered at several stages and in diverse manner, various part of the Indian subcontinent, comprising different ethnic groups, political systems and religious beliefs. However, under the aegis of the Indian National Congress and since 1920, under the leadership of Mahatma Gandhi, these various ethnic and religious elements, came together against foreign colonial rule and developed a consciousness of nationhood. Unfortunately, this common struggle against foreign imperialism, that has welded these diverse people in the Indian subcontinent into one nation, did not somehow have an appreciable impact on the Nagas. This was, no doubt, due to the policy of isolation and exclusion, so deftly practiced by the British rulers, who believed in creating pockets contrary to each other and hoping to rule in perpetuity by dividing the peoples. In any case, this great national movement of unification which freed India including Nagaland from the yoke of foreign rule, did not bring within its embracing sweep the Naga population to the same extent as it did the other parts of the subcontinent. Thus in 1947, when all the diverse people of India

who had been brought under British rule, voluntarily agreed to form the Union of India and to share in the common endeavour to ensure that in this great Union the ideals of Fraternity, Liberty, Justice and Equality, as enshrined in the Constitution are fully achieved, for the common benefit of all, the same reasons and sense of participation was not noticeable in the Naga areas.

13. The Peace Mission, in the circumstances, appreciates and understands their urge to preserve their integrity. The Peace Mission also appreciates the courage and tenacity displayed by the Naga people in their endeavour to achieve this goal., The objective which they may have placed before themselves in their memorandum "Naga Peace Delegation" dated 17 December 1964 and addressed to the Peace Mission, namely their desire to find peace, their resolve to maintain their integrity and to resist entanglement in war, all extremely laudable and should commend themselves to all peace-loving people. It is, however, to be noted that this Declaration, in itself, does not resolve the political issue. Therefore, some appropriate meeting point as to be found, where the aims and ideals of the NFG can be achieved, at the same time making it possible for the Government of India to accept these within the framework of the political settlement to be mutually agreed upon.

14. The Peace Mission in the pursuit of a settlement through peaceful means, to which the Government of India as well as the NFG to consider seriously whether such meeting point could not be reached. On the one hand, the NFG could on their own volition, decide to be a participant in the Union of India and mutually settle the terms and conditions for the purpose. On the other hand, the Government of India could consider to what

extent the pattern and structure of the relationship between Nagaland and the Government of India should be adopted and recast; so as to satisfy the political aspirations of all sections of Naga opinion and to make it possible for the ideals of peace as expressed in the Naga Peace Declaration to be substantially realised.

15. The Peace Mission would like, in all earnestness, to impress upon both sides that the approach, herein suggested, is not only the fairest, but the only practical one in the given circumstances: and it fervently hopes that it will commend itself to the Government of India as well as to the Nagaland Federal Government.

16. The Peace Mission reiterates that the peace now obtaining in Nagaland should be made everlasting. With that object in view, the Peace Mission offered certain suggestions, whereupon both the parties had unequivocally affirmed and declared that they would renounce war and violence as a means for political settlement. This declaration of renunciation of war and use of armed force, it is earnestly emphasised, must not be deviated from by any means. The Peace Mission's Proposal following this bilateral Declaration of Renunciation of war, to deposit all underground arms in safe custody and to withdraw all Indian security forces from law and order duties could not unfortunately be implemented.

17. Nevertheless, the Peace Mission would earnestly desire that, in faithful pursuance of the Declaration of Renunciation of use of armed force, both parties take concrete steps to remove all frictions. There have been numerous complaints and counter complaints from both. The Peace Mission would suggest that the NFG require all arms issued to its force to be concentrated at one or several places, in their armories

and under their custody so that there can be no basis of any future complaints of their forces parading with arms or extorting money or supplies under threat. They should also seriously ask themselves whether recruiting and movements out of Nagaland towards Pakistan do not create an impression that these are only acts preparatory towards resumption of hostilities and, if so, they should take remedial measures by putting a stop to such recruitment and movement. The Government of India should instruct its armed forces and the civil administration to continue to abide strictly by the terms of the Agreement, both in spirit and letter.

18. The Peace Mission makes a fervent appeal for consideration of the suggestions contained in this paper and for all action that is possible for the maintenance of peace.

Date: 20 December, 1964.

Sd/-

1. Bimala Prasad Chaliha
2. Jayaprakash Narayan
3. Michael Scott

The Shilong Accord of 11 November 1975 between the Government of India and the Underground Nagas

The following representative of the underground organization met the Governor of Nagaland Shri. L.P. Singh, representing the Government of India, at Shillong on 10 and 11 November 1975.

1. Shri. I. Temjenba
2. Shri. S. Dahru
3. Shri. Veenyiyi Rhakhu
4. Shri. Z. Ramyo
5. Shri. M. Assa
6. Shri. Kevi Yallay

1. There was a series of four discussions. Some of the discussions were held with the Governor alone; at others, the Governor was assisted by the two Advisers for Nagaland, Shri. Ramunny and Shri. H. Zopianga, and Shri. M.L. Kampani, Joint Secretary in the Ministry of Home Affairs. All the five members of the Liaison Committee namely Rev. Longri Ao, Dr. M. Aram, Shri. L. Lungalang, Shri Kennith

Kerhuo and Shri. Lungshim Shaiza, participated in the discussions.

3. The following were the outcomes of the discussions:
   (i) The representatives of the underground organizations convoyed their decision, of their own volition, to accept, without condition, the Constitution of India;
   (ii) It was agreed that the arms, now underground, would be brought out and deposited at appointed places. Details for giving effect to this agreement will be worked out between them and representative of the government, the security for and members of the Liaison Committee;
   (iii) It was agreed that the representatives of the underground organizations should have reasonable time to formulate other issues for discussion for final settlement.

Dated, Shillong
11 November 1975

I. TEMJENBA; S. DEHRU
Z. RAMYO; M. ASSA
KEVI YALLAY
On behalf of the representatives of
Underground organizations.

LP. SINGH
On behalf of the
Government of India

Annexure 'G'
Supplementary Agreement to the Shilong Accord on 5 January 1976

Implementation of clause II of the Shillong Accord of 11 November 1975.

1. It was decided that the collection of arms initially at collection centres, would commence as early as possible, and will be completed by 25 January 1976. Initial places of collection to be decided through discussion between Commissioners, representatives of underground organizations and the members of the Liaison Committee.
2. Once all arms are collected, these will be handed over to Peace Council team at the respective places of collections.
3. Peace Council team will arrange to transport the arms from collection centres to Chedema Peace Camp and arrange guards, etc, for safe custody of arm.
4. Similar arrangement at agreed place/places will be made in Manipur with concurrence of the Manipur Government.
5. The underground may stay at Peace camps to be established at suitable place, and their maintenance will be arranged only by the Peace Council. Any voluntary contribution from any source will be made

to Peace Council, who will utilize the fund according to necessity.

Biseto Medom Keyho; Pukrove Nakru;	L.P. Singh
Z. Ramyo; I. Temjenba	Governor

Dated, Shillong
5 January 1976.

Armed Forces (Special Power) Act, 1958 (As amended in 1972)

An Act to enable certain special powers to be conferred upon members of the Armed Forces in disturbed areas in States of ASSAM, MANIPUR, MEGHALAYA, NAGALAND AND TRIPURA and the UNION TERRITORIES of ARUNACHAL and MIZORAM. Be it enacted by Parliament in the Ninth Year of the Republic of India as follows:

1. (i) This Act may be called the Armed Forces (Special Power) Act, 1958.

   (ii) It extends to the whole of the States of Assam, Manipur, Meghalaya, Nagaland and Tripura and the Union Territories of Arunachal Pradesh and Mizoram.

2. In this Act, unless the context otherwise requires.

   (a) "Armed Forces" means the military and the Air Force of the Union so operating;

   (b) "Disturbed Area" mean an area which is for the time being declared by notification under Section 3 to be disturbed area;

   (c) All other words and expressions used herein, but not defined in the Air force Act, 1950, or in the Army Act, 1950, shall have the meanings respectively assigned to them in those Acts.

3. If in relation any to State or Union Territory to which this Act extends, the Governor of the State, or the Administrator of the Union Territory, or the Central Government in either case: is of the opinion that the whole or any is in such a disturbed or dangerous condition that the use of Armed forces in aid of civil power is necessary, the Governor of that State or the Administrator of that Union Territory of the Central Government as the case may be, may, by notification in the Official Gazette declares the whole or such part of such State or Union Territory to be a disturbed areas.
4. Any commissioned officer, warrant officer, non-commissioned office or any other person of equivalent rank in the Armed Forces may, in a disturb area,
   (a) if he is of opinion that it is necessary to do so for maintenance of public order, after giving such due warning as he may consider necessary, fire upon or otherwise us force, even to the causing of death, against any person who is acting in contravention of any law or order for the time being in the disturbed area prohibiting the assembly of five or more persons or the carrying of weapons or of things capable of being used as weapons of fire-arms, ammunition or explosive substances;
   (b) if he is of opinion that it is necessary to do so, destroy any arms dump, prepared or fortified position or shelter from which armed attacks are made or are likely to be made or are attempted to be made, or any structure used as a training camp for armed volunteers or utilize as a hide-out by armed gangs or absconders wanted for any offence;
   (c) Arrest, without warrant, any person who has committed a cognizable offence or against whom a

reasonable suspicion exists that he has committed or is about to commit a cognizable offence and such force as may be necessary to affect the arrest;

(d) enter and search without warrant, any premises to make any such arrest as aforesaid or to recover any person believed to be wrongfully restrained or confined to be stolen property or any arms, ammunition or explosive substances believed to be unlawfully kept in such premises: and may for that purpose use force as may be necessary.

5. Any person arrested and taken into custody under this Act shall be made over to the officer in charge of the nearest police station with the least possible delay, together with a report of the circumstances occasioning the arrest.

6. No prosecution, suit or other legal proceeding shall be instituted, except with the previous sanction of the Central Government against any person in respect of anything done or purported to be done in exercise of powers conferred by this Act.

Bibliography

A. PRIMARY SOURCES

(i) Government Published Documents

1. Government of Manipur, Administrative Report 1919-20, 1970-86.
2. Government of Manipur, (Directorate of Economics and Statistics) *Manipur At-A-Glance,* District wise 1986.
3. Government of Manipur, *Handbook of Manipur Hill Village Authority,* 1956.
4. Government of Manipur, (Directorate of Tribal Development and Backward Classes) *Tribals in Manipur At-A-Glance,* 1987.
5. Government of Manipur, (Office of the Chief Electoral Officer) Result of the first elections in Manipur State 1953, 1957, 1962.
6. Government of Manipur, *Manipur To-Day* Independence Day Special Issue, 1987.

(ii) Articles, Magazines, and Journals etc.

1. *The Naga Monthly Magazine,* published by K. Prongo, Imphal, 1981.
2. *Naga Students Federation Magazine,* Ist issue 1981-83 Vol : I and 111981, Kohima.
3. *Tangkhul Katamnao Saklong Riyan* (constitution) Ukhiul.

4. *Jadonang a Challenge to British Imperialism*, Raj.
5. *Rethinking about the Strategy of Tribal Development* by Burman B.K. Roy.
6. *Rani Gaidinlu,*, Amit, Kumar Nag, Silchal 1976.
7. *Jadonang* (A Freedom fighter of Manipur Commemorative Vol: on the occasion of Jadonang 41 death Anniversary, 29 August 1971, Imphal.
8. *Commemorative Publication on the Changing Political and Demographic Trends in North East India.* Department of Political Science Manipur University 1985.
9. *Naga Seed-Sowing Festival*, All Naga Student's Union Manipur Imphal. 1987.
10. *A Souvenir. The Naga Seed Sowing Festival* published by ANSUM Imphal 1987.
11. *A Souvenir, Nagas 90,* published by Literature Committee Nagas 90-1990.
12. *A Souvenir, A Question of Human Rights,* Imphal, 1990.
13. *Zeliangrong Movement 1927-1977: A Brief History* by Gangumei Kamei Resistance January 10, 1987, Imphal.
14. *Seeds of the Naga Question* Resistance, January 18, 1978 (a report carried by Shillong Times dated December 5, 1947).
15. *After Khonoma,* Resistance, May 16, 1978, Imphal, p.5.
16. *Journal of the North Eastern Council,* Shillong, October December, 1990, Vol: XI No. 4.
17. *The North Eastern Research Bulletin,* Vol-V Summer 1974, V V Rao articles on -North East India: Problems and suggestions.
18. Souvenir—The Third Annual Conference, North East India History Association, December 6-8, 1982, Manipur University, Imphal, Dr. M. Horam's articles, *The Nagas of the North East India: Aveneral View.*
19. *Regional Integration*, Vol-XI No. 1 March 1986, Imphal.

20. Regional Integration, Vol-X No. 1 June 1985, *Head Hunting,* by YK. Shimray.
21. Regional Integration, Vol. No I June 1985, *Hill administration of Manipur,* S. Mangi Singh.
22. *Naga Politics* by M. Horam, Paper present in Seminar organised by Naga Student's Union, Delhi.
23. *Identity Crises in the Changing Society* by K. Prongo, Imphal.
24. *The Crises in Naga politics,* by Dr. Viseer Sangu, on 13 th NSF General conference, Tsemenyu, 1989.
25. *Nature of Administration in Manipur and Nagaland,* (Pre-Independence Period) by Dr. Ksh. Bimol Devi, Paper present in Seminar sponsored by UGC, Imphal 1989.
26. *Constraints of Economic Development,* A Study on Manipur. Hills, by Ashok Kumar Ray, Paper present on Seminar sponsored by UGC, Imphal, 1989.
27. Aram, M., *Social Change and Political Tension in Nagaland,* North-Eastern Research Bulletin 3 Summer, 30-3 8.
28. *Bilateral Monoloque* (Talk between Government and the Nagas leaders) Economic and Political weekly October 14, 1947 (Editorial).
29. Das Gupta, Barun, (1967) *For permanent Peace in Nagaland,* Mainstream, January 26, pp. 57-58.
30. Das Gupta, Panalal, *Wither Nagaland,* Mainstream, 1968, June 1, June 15, June 22, June 29, articles.
31. Malik, Jarji, Nagaland: *A Search for Identity,* Times Weekly, September 17, 1972, pp. 1, 3.]
32. *Naga Factions,* Link-1968, January 23, pp. 25-26, 70.
33. Lolly R. R: *The Baptist Church in Manipur,* (Historical Survey), Imphal, 1985.
34. *An Open Letter to Naga Friends,* The Weekly Journal vol. I No. 47, March 28, 1990.

35. *The Naga have a dream higher than hope* - The Kaphungkhon, Vol. 5, March 1990, Imphal (editor).
36. *Republic Dav Speech,* 21st March 1991, Isak Chisi Swu. Chairman National Socialist Council of Nagaland.
37. *The NSCN Manifesto and Polarisation,* published by government of the people's Republic of Nagaland, 1980.
38. *Phizo's Last Journey to Nagaland,* Sun Magazine, Vol, XIII No. 42, May 19, 1990.
39. *Underground Outfit Join Hands* Sun Magazine, Vol, <CIV No. 2, August 11, 1990.
40. *Armv Rides Again,* Sun Magazine Vol. XIV No. 48, May 4, 1991.
41. *India "Operation Bluebird" A Case Study U:* Torture and *Extrajudicial Executions in Manipur.* Amnesty International International Secretariat lesion Street, London WCIX 8 D J United Kingdom, October 1990.
42. *Nagas at work* Naga Students Union Delhi, Delhi 1996.

(iii) News Paper Articles

1. Chopra, Maharaja K *'Problem of Nagaland, Indian Expressed,* January 11, 1967, p. 6.
2. Choras, 'Lack of Co-ordination in Dealing with Naga Rebels', *Statesman,* June 18, 1968, p. 6(Article).
3. Das A.N. 'From Armed Insurgency to Peace in North East Region', Amrita *Bazar* Patrika May 2-4, 1967.
4. Jagiani, J. A., Nagaland', *Indian Express.* February 25, 1967 (Editorial).
5. Khanna, K.C., 'Two Faces of Nagaland, An Uncertain Future', *Times of India,* October 19, 1967, p,8.
6. Mukherjee Dilip, 'Search for Stability along Eastern Frontier', *Statesmen,* March 1, 1968, P.6 (Article).

7. Fifth Round (Talks with underground Naga Leaders)' *Times of India* January 7, 1967 (editorial).
8. 'Naga Fiacso', *Times of India.* October 22, 1967, p. 8.
9. Naga Question', *Times of India,* January 15, 1967, p.8.
10. Naga Rebels', *Hindu,* October, 21 1967, p.6. (editorial).
11. Nagaland', *Hindustan Times,* June 14, 1967, p.9 (editorial).
12. 'Tribes on the Run', *Statesman,* July 15, 1976.
13. '100 Underground Nagas on Burma-Nagaland Border'. *Hindu,* May 16, 1976.
14. Waiting for Phizo (Naga Problem)', *Statesman,* June 10, 1967.
15. 'How Long wrill the North-East Tribals Live off Charity?' Pradip Phanjaobam, *Times of India,* September 8, 1989.

(iv) Person Interviewed

1. Ringshi Keishing - Ex-Serviceman (Now Pastor).
2. V Khosapa - Student.
3. Wunghim Angkan - Lecturer.
4. Fillson Lunghar -Student Leader.
5. Rocky Khumlao - Contractor.
6. Daniel Ramson -Advocate.
7. H. Khangam - Farmer.
8. Wonmi Ragui – Student
9. Shimther Horam - Village Headman.
10. K. Envy - Politician (Ex-MP).

(v) Other Publication:

1. The Yehzabo of Nagaland (Constitution).
2. The Nine-Point Agreement, June 1947.
3. The 16-Point Agreement arrived at between the Government of India and the Naga People's Convention, July 1960.

4. Shillong Accord, between the Government of India and Underground Nagas, November 11, 1975.

B. GAZETTERS

1. Allen B.C., *Gazetteers of the Naga Hills and Manipr. xr.* 1906.
2. Allen B. C., *Gazetteer of the Naga Hills of Manipur,* (.ks s a m District), Gazetteer Vol. IX, 1905.
3. Dun, W.H. *Gazetteer of Manipur,* Vivek Publishing House, Delhi, 1975.
4. Bareh, H., *Gazetteer of India,* Nagaland, Kohima District, Calcutta, 1970.
5. Sıngh, K.B. *Census of India,* 1961, Vol. XXII, Manipur Part V-A.

C. SECONDARY SOURCES:

1. Aram M.: *Peace in Nagaland, New* Delhi, 1974.
2. Anand, Maj V K: *Nagaland in Transition,* New Delhi, 1967.
3. Alemchaba AO : *A Brief Historicat account of Nagaland,* Kohima, 1972.
4. Alice Taylor: *South East Asia* (ed), 1972.
5. Bashan, A. L. : *The Wonder that was India.* London, 1954.
6. Bhattacharya, Ajitkumar : *Political Evolution of Nagaland.* Calcutta Book Trust (1945-65).
7. Bower, Arsula: *The Naga Path,* London John Murray, 1950.
8. Barpujari H. K. : *Problem of the Hill Tribes North-East Frontier* 1822-42 Vol. I Lawers Book Stall, Guahati, 1970.
9. Parpujari H.K. : *Problems of the Hill Tribes North-East Frontiers 1973-1962,* Vol. III Spectrum Publication, Guahati, 1981.
10. Butler, Captain J.: *Administration Reports of the Naga Hills,* 1870-1871, Calcutta. 1871.

11. Chakroborty BC : *British Relations with the Hills Tribes of Assam* since 1964.
12. Chandrika Singh : *Political Evolution of Idagalaixd,* No, Delhi, 1981.
13. Chaobe, S.K.: *Hill Politics in North_ East India,* Orient Longman, Delhi, 1978.
14. Dena, Lal : *British Policy Towards Manipur 1891-1919,* Imphal, 1984.
15. Desai, A.R. : *Social Background of India Nationalism* Bombay, 1948.
16. Downs, F.S.: *The Christianity in North East India, Christia;* Literature.
17. Elwin, V. : *Nagaland,* Shillong, 1961.
18. Elwin, V. : *Nagas in the Nineteenth Century,* Oxford University Press, London, 1964.
19. Elwin V. : *Indias North-East Frontier in the Nineteenth Century* Oxford University Press, 1959.
20. Ghosh, B.B.: *History of Nagaland,* Delhi, 1982.
21. Gundevia, Y.D.: *War and Peace in Nagaland* Delhi, 1975.
22. Hodson, T.C. : The Naga Tribes of Manipur, B. R. Publication Corporation, Dehi, 1982.
23. Haimendorf, Ch. V. Furer : *Tribes of India Struggle for Survival*, Oxford University Press, New Delhi, 1982.
24. Haimendorf, Ch. V. Furer: *The Naked Nagas,* Calcutta, 1962.
25. Horam, M. : *Naga Polity,* B. R. Publishing Corporation, Delhi 1975.
26. Horam, M. : *Social and Cultural Life of Nagas*, B.R. Publishing, Delhi, 1977.
26. Horam, M.: *Naga Insurgency*, Cosmo Publication, Delhi, 1988.
27. Horam, M.: *North-East India A Profile*, Cosmo Publication, Delhi, 1990.

28. Horam Ringkahao: *The Genesis of the Naga political movement*, enjoys publication, Imphal 1998.

29. Hutton, J.H. : *The Angami Nagas*, Mac, Millan & Co. Ltd., London, 1981.

30. Hutton, J.H.: *Report on Naga Hills*, Mittal Publication, Delhi, 1986.

31. Jain MP: *Political Theory*, Authors build Publications, Delhi, 1979.

32. Johnstone, J.: *My Experience in Manipur and Naga Hills*, London, 1896.

33. Jonstone, J. : *Manipur and the Naga Tribes*, Minas Publication, Delhi, 1987.

34. Kaka D Iralu: *Nagaland and India*, 2000.

35. Kamei Gangmumei: *Jadonang, A Mystic Naga Rebel*, 1997.

36. Keane AH: *Asia with ethnological appendix*, Vol. II, London.

37. King James Version: *Holy Bible,* Identity Seafield World Publishing USA.

38. Kongyak, H.Y.: *From Darkness to Light*, Guahati, 1990.

39. Lewis S Fever: *Ideology and the Ideologists*, Western Printing services Ltd. Oxford 1975.

40. Lord, M.A.: *Missionaries and Education in Bengal*, 1793-1837, Oxford, 1873.

41. Mackenzie, A.: *History of the Relations of the Government with the Hill Tribes of the North East Frontier of Bengal*, Calcutta, 1884.

42. Mankekar, D.K.: *On the Slippery Slope in Nagaland*, Manaktalas, Bombay, 1967.

43. Marx Karl: *The Class struggles in France* (1848-50) ed. CP Dutt (New York).

44. Mark N Hagopian: *Regime Movements and Ideologies Longman*, New York, 1970.

45. Mills, J.P.: *The Lhota Naga*, London, 1922.
46. Mills, J.P.: *The Ao Naga*, London, 1926.
47. Mills, J.P.: *The Rengma Naga*, London, 1937.
48. Mills, J.P. Moifall: *Report on the Province of Assam*, 1854.
49. Mullik BN: *My year with Nehru*, 1948-64, Delhi 1972.
50. Murkot Ramunny: *The World of Nagas*, Northern Book Centre, Delhi, 1988.
51. Naga Institute of Culture: *The Arts and Crafts of Nagaland*, Calcutta, 1968.
52. Namo Dalle: *The Prisoner from Nagaland*, Guahati, 1987.
53. Nandita Haksar & Luingam Luithui: *Nagaland File Lancer International*, Delhi,1984.
54. Nibedon Nirmal: *Nagaland the Night of the Guerrillas.*
55. NNC: *The Naga National Rights and Movement*, 1993.
56. Pemberton RB: *The Eastern Frontier of India* Mittal Publications, Delhi – 59, 2000.
57. Pettergrew, W.: *Forty Years in Manipur*, Assam, March, 1934, 1st Print in India, Imphal, 1936.
58. Pettegrew, W.: *Tangkhul Naga Grammar*, Shillong, 1918.
59. Philip, P.T.: *The Growth of the Baptist Church in Nagaland*, Christian Literature Centre, Guahati, 1976.
60. Phizo, A.Z.: *The Fate of the Nagas*, An Appeal to the World, London, 1960.
61. Ray Amal and Bhattarcharya: *Political Theory. The World Press*, Private Ltd. Calcutta 1989.
62. Reid Robert: *History of the Frontier Areas Bordering on Assam from 1883-1941*, Shillong, 1942.
63. Robertson David: *Dictionary of Politics*, Penguin Publication, London, 1985.
64. Roland Shimmi: *Comparative History of the Nagas*, Inter-India Publication, Delhi, 1988.

65. Rustomji, N.: *Enchanting Frontier*, London, 1971.
66. Rev. Nuh, V.K.: *My Country My People*, Published by Chakeshang Student's Union, 1988.
67. Scott Rev. Mechael: *The Nagas: India's problem or the World's the Search for peace*, London, 1966.
68. Sema Hokeshe: *Emergency of Nagaland*, Vikas Publishing House Pvt., 1986.
69. Sen Sepra: *Tribes and Castes of Manipur*, Mittal Publications Delhi 1992.
70. Shimray, R.R.: *Origin and Culture of Nagas*, New Delhi, 1984.
71. Shakspeare L.W.: *History of upper Assam, Upper Burma and North Eastern Forntier*. London Macmillen and company 1914.
72. Shishak Yangmasho: *II World War in Manipur, 1944*. Ukhrul, Manipur. Personal Publication 1996.
73. Singh, K.S.: *Tribal Movement in India*, Vol. I, Manohar Publication, Delhi, 1982.
74. Singh, Prakash: *Nagaland*, National Book Trust, New Delhi, 1972-79.
75. Singh, Randhir, K: *The Nagas of Nagaland*, Deep and Deep Publication, Delhi, 1987.
76. Stracy, P.D. : *Nagaland Nightmare*, Bombay, 1968.
77. Sumi V.D. Timothy K.: *Cry for Justice*, Revised Edition 1997 by Ministry of Information and Publicity, GPRN.
78. Tagore, D.: *Israel in India*, 1986.
79. Taylor Alice: *South East Asia* (ed), 1972.
80. Vaiphei, Prim: *Church Growth among the Hills Tribes in Manipur, North-East India*, Press, Imphal, 1986.
81. Wati Aier: *A Cry from the Rice Fields*, (A Call Freedom for the Nagas) Dimapur, 1989.
83. Yunou Asoso: *The Rising Nagas*, New Delhi, 1974.

83. Yunou Asoso: *Nagas Struggles against British Rule under Jadonang and Rani Gaidinlu*, 1925-1947, Kohima, 1982.

84. Zarkman IW and Berman MR: *The Practical Negotiator*, New Haven, Yale University Press, 1982.

85. Zenyu M: *Phizo and the Naga problem*, Nagaland Times Press, Dimapur, 1979.